GODS OF TIN

GODS OF TIN

∾

The Flying Years

JAMES SALTER

∾

EDITED AND SELECTED BY

Jessica Benton and William Benton

Shoemaker & Hoard
Washington, D.C.

Library of Congress Cataloging-in-Publication Data
Salter, James.
Gods of tin : the flying years / James Salter ; edited and selected by Jessica Benton and William Benton.
ISBN 1−59376−006-x
p. cm.
Includes bibliographical references and index.
1. Salter, James—Diaries. 2. Air pilots, Military—United States—Anecdotes. 3. Korean war, 1950−1953—Aerial operations—Anecdotes. I. Benton, Jessica. II. Benton, William, 1939− III. Title.
TL540.S183A3   2004
813′.54—dc22   2004011664

Book design by Mark McGarry, Texas Type & Book Works
Set in Requiem

Printed in the United States of America

Shoemaker $\boxed{\substack{\text{S}\& \\ \text{H}}}$ Hoard
A Division of Avalon Publishing Group Inc.
Distributed by Publishers Group West

10 9 8 7 6 5 4 3 2 1

GODS OF TIN

THE FLYING YEARS

FOREWORD

James Salter is one of the important writers of our time. He is the author of six novels, among them *Light Years,* and *A Sport and a Pastime* which was selected as a title in The Modern Library in 1995. His collection of short stories, *Dusk,* won the Pen/Faulkner Award in 1998, and in 2000 he was elected to the American Academy of Arts and Letters. Yet before he was a novelist, he was a fighter pilot in the Air Force, a graduate of West Point who flew over one hundred missions during the Korean War. In his memoir *Burning the Days* (1997), he describes the difficult decision to resign from the military in midcareer and begin another life. "It was in me like a pathogen—the idea of being a writer." But the pathogen—or passion—of flying is no less ineradicable in the literary man. The courage, risk, and self-measure of the one become a standard for the other, transmuted into the writer's style, and nowhere are the deft and minute tunings of Salter's prose more evident than when he writes about his experiences in the air.

The text of this book has been compiled from *The Hunters* (1956), Salter's first novel, set in Korea during the war, where he was stationed from February to August of 1952; from *Cassada* (2000), a reworking of an earlier novel, *The Arm of Flesh* (1961), which deals with a squadron in Europe a few years after Korea; and from the "flight years" of *Burning the Days*. It also includes, published here for the first time, many sections of a journal Salter kept during the Korean War. It is, as a record of the day-to-day, mission-to-mission life of a young fighter pilot, a remarkable document by any standards. But it provides as well a view into the crucible of a writer's beginnings, like pencil studies that precede a painting, in which the essential qualities of the artist's hand are unmistakable.

> *20 April 1952.* First morning mission. Weather not good. Near Pyongyang shreds of cirrus hung in the air like icicles on the edge of a roof. Ahead, the mist was flat as a table. A band of green haze rimmed the distant horizon.

The overall structure of the book is made up of passages from all four sources strung together chronologically, and divided into four main sections. The parts bind together to create a coherent whole that resembles, perhaps more than anything else, a modern, Homeric poem. In *Burning the Days*, subtitled *A Recollection*, the personal details of the author's life were revealed obliquely, through stories. *Gods of Tin*—the tin is aircraft—stripped of narrative connections and including both fiction and nonfiction, reads like unabashed autobiography. A life is in front of you, with human vulnerability and heroic reach.

War, like love and death, is without an equivalent experience. In one passage, Salter writes:

> You lived and died alone, especially in fighters. Fighters. Somehow, despite everything, that word had not become sterile. You slipped into the hollow cockpit and strapped and plugged yourself into the machine. The canopy ground shut and sealed you off. Your oxygen, your very breath, you carried with you into the chilled vacuum, in a steel bottle.

WILLIAM BENTON

It was said of Lord Byron that he was more proud of his Norman ancestors who had accompanied William the Conqueror in the invasion of England than of having written famed works. The name de Burun, not yet Anglicized, was inscribed in the Domesday book. Looking back, I feel a pride akin to that in having flown and fought along the Yalu.

FROM THE AUTHOR'S PREFACE TO *THE HUNTERS*

I.

By the summer of 1942, America had been at war with Japan and Germany for more than half a year. James Salter, following in the footsteps of his father who had attended twenty-five years earlier, entered the military academy at West Point. He had just turned seventeen.

In mid-July up the steep road from the station we walked as a group. I knew no one. Like the others I carried a small suitcase in which would be put the clothes I would not see again for years. We passed large, silent buildings and crossed a road beneath some trees. A few minutes later, having signed a consent paper, we stood in the hall in a harried line trying to memorize a sentence to be used in reporting to the cadet first sergeant. It had to be spoken loudly and exactly. Failure meant going out and getting back in line to do it again. There was constant shouting and beyond the door of the barracks an ominous noise, alive, that flared when the door was opened like the roar of a furnace. It was the din of the Area, upperclassmen, some bellowing, some whispering, some hissing like snakes. They were giving the same commands over and over as they stalked the nervous ranks that stood stiffly at attention, still in civilian clothes, already forbidden to look anywhere but straight ahead. The air was rabid. The heat poured down ...

It is the sounds I remember, the iron orchestra, the feet on the stairways, the clanging bells, the shouting, cries of *Yes, No, I do not know, sir!*, the clatter of sixty or seventy rifle butts as they came down on the pavement at nearly the same time. Life was anxious minutes, running everywhere, scrambling to formations ...

First day at West Point

All was tradition, the language, the gray woolen cloth, the high black collars of the dress coats, the starched white pants that you got into standing on a chair. Always in summer the Corps had lived in tents out on the Plain, under canvas, with duckboard streets—Summer Camp with its fraternal snapshots and first classmen lounging against tent poles; this was among the few things that had disappeared. There was the honor system, about which we heard from the very beginning, which belonged to the cadets rather than to the authorities and had as its most severe punishment "silencing." Someone who was guilty of a violation and refused to resign could be silenced, never spoken to by his classmates except officially for the rest of his life. He was made to room by himself, and one of the few acknowledgements of his existence was at a dance—if he appeared everyone walked from the floor, leaving him, the girl, and the orchestra all alone. Even his pleasures were quarantined.

∾

West Point was a keep of tradition and its name was a hallmark. It drew honest, Protestant, often rural, and largely uncomplicated men—although there were figures like Poe, Whistler, and even Robert E. Lee, who later said that getting a military education had been the greatest mistake of his life.

I remember the sweating, the heat and thirst, the banned bliss of long gulping from the spigot. At parades, three or four a week, above the drone of hazing floated the music of the band. It seemed part of another, far-off world. There was the feeling of being on a hopeless journey, an exile that would last for years. In the distance, women in light frocks strolled with officers, and the fine house of the Superintendent gleamed toylike and white. In the terrific sun someone in the next rank or beside you begins to sway, take an involuntary step, and like a beaten fighter fall forward. Rifles litter the ground. Afterwards a tactical officer walks among them as among bodies on a battlefield, noting down the serial numbers.

∽

I was undergoing a conversion, from a self divided and consciously inferior, as William James described it, to one that was unified and, to use his word, right. I saw myself as the heir of many strangers, the faces of those who had gone before, my new roommate's brother, for one, John Eckert, who had graduated two years earlier and was now a medium bomber pilot in England. I had a photograph of him and his wife, which I kept in my desk, the pilot with his rakish hat, the young wife, the clarity of their features, the distinction. Perhaps it was in part because of this snapshot that I thought of becoming a pilot. At least it was one more branch thrown onto the pyre. When he was killed on a mission not long after, I felt a secret thrill and envy. His life, the scraps I knew of it, seemed worthy, complete. He had left something behind, a woman who could never forget him; I had her picture. Death seemed the purest act. Comfortably distant from it I had no fear.

∽

Salter as a second-year cadet with his mother

The army, at that time, included what would later become the
Air Force, and pilots and aircrews, as well as those supporting
them, were members of the army.

ത

There was a special physical examination in the winter of 1944
that included the eyes: aligning two pegs in a sort of lighted
shoebox by pulling strings—"Am I good enough for the Air
Corps, sir?"—and identifying colors by picking up various balls
of yarn. In April, those who passed, hundreds, that is, including my two roommates and me, went off to flight training in
the South and Southwest. Hardly believing our good fortune,
we went as if it were a holiday, by train. Left behind were
classes, inspections, and many full-dress parades. Ahead was
freedom and the joy of months away.

ത

I was linking everything together, fatalism, sex, war. In my
imagination I was already a pilot, handsome, freedom reeking
from me, winds coiled round my legs. I had no real idea of what
lay ahead, vast southwestern skies with their clouds and shafts
of light, towns with railroad tracks running through them and
Masonic lodges, dejected country with little lakes and fading
cabins amid the pines, Bible country, the air pure with poverty
and religious broadcasts. It didn't matter, I was going.

∽

Pine Bluff, Arkansas, on a loop of a sluggish, curving river, was where we learned to fly. The field was east of town. The flying school there was run by civilians.

We lived in barracks and were broken up into flights—four students to an instructor—alphabetically, of course, although inexplicably I was together with Marlow, Milnor, and Mahl. Our instructor was an ancient, perhaps in his forties, crop duster from a town in the southwest part of the state, Hope, which he described as the watermelon capital of the world. His name was Basil York.

∽

Early flights, the instructor in the rear cockpit, the bumpy taxiing on the grass, turning into the wind, tail swinging around, dust blowing, and then the abrupt, wild sound of the engine. The ground was speeding by, the wheels skipping, and suddenly we were rising in the din to see the blue tree line beyond the field boundary and, below, the curved roofs of the hangers falling away. Now fields appeared, swimming out in all directions. The earth became limitless, the horizon, unseen before, rose to fill the world and we were aloft in unstructured air.

Looking over the side of the airplane, I could not believe it, the noise, the clatter of the engine, the battering wind, and the

PT-19, primary trainer, the first airplane flown

flat country below laid out in large rectangular patterns with dirt roads, the glint of occasional metal roofs, smooth water. They talked meaninglessly about "section lines." In the air these quickly became real.

We passed a thousand feet. I felt as helpless as if sitting in a chair at that height. We climbed higher, to fifteen hundred or two thousand feet, the height of the stalls, the first demonstrated maneuvers. The nose soars up into steep blue air, higher, higher still, unforgivingly higher, something sickening is happening, the bottom of the seat feels ready to drop away, and the dry voice of the instructor is explaining it as at the top the plane, almost motionless, suddenly shudders, then starts to fall. Now I am to do this, his matter-of-fact voice directing it:

throttle back, pull the nose up, way up, higher, hold it there, hold it . . .

There were spins, jamming the rudder in at the top of a stall and falling, the plane turning around and around like a maple pod. There was the anguish of trying to make proper "S" turns across a road, the wind making one loop bigger than the other unless you steepened your bank.

An hour has passed. All directions have melted away, the earth is too vast and confusing to be able to say where we are. Only later it is clear that the roads run on cardinal headings, north-south, east-west. The world and everything in it, the river, farmers' houses, the roads and lone cars, are unaware of us, droning above. The field is nowhere in sight. Like a desert, everything visible is almost the same when he says, "OK. Take us home." It must be this way, you think, though there is nothing to confirm it. After a few minutes, without a word, he brusquely corrects the heading ninety degrees as if in disgust.

Everything you have done has been unsatisfactory, the stalls not steep enough, the "S" turns uneven, the nose of the plane continually wandering off in one direction or the other when you are told to hold it straight and level, anything that could speed up, slide, or drift away has done so.

In the distance, magically, the field appears and with precision, sometimes explaining what he is doing, he enters the traffic pattern and expertly lands. My flying suit is black with sweat.

Face glazed, disheartened, I scramble from the plane as soon as we park. One of the others is standing there to take my place.

∽

All was tin, the corrugated hangars shining in the sun, the open-cockpit airplanes, the tin gods. We were expected to solo in a few hours, not less than four or more than eight. If you were not able to take off and land by yourself after eight hours, you were washed out. The days were filled with classes, briefings, flights, the sound of planes, the smell of them. We were mixed in with regular air cadets, some of whom were older and had flown before. We marched with them, singing their songs, the vulgarity of which was disarming, and continued to kick into spins at three thousand feet on every flight and mechanically chant the formula: throttle off, stick forward, pause, opposite rudder . . . Even after three or four flights I still did not fully understand what a chandelle was supposed to be and had only a faint conception of a landing.

Like the first buds appearing, individuals began to solo. Word of who had done it spread immediately. Face scorched red by the sun, in the back cockpit Basil York repeated over and over the desiderata as we entered traffic, "Twenty-fifty and five hundred, twenty-fifty and five hundred." He was referring to engine rpm and traffic pattern altitude. "When you're flying B-17s," he said in his high-pitched voice, "I want you to still be hearing that: twenty-fifty and five hundred." We had begun to execute the landings together, nose up, throttle all the way off, both of us on the stick. I knew his recitation, "Start breaking the glide, ease back on the throttle, start rounding out, all right, that's good, hold it off now, hold it off . . ." The trouble was, I did not know what it all meant.

∽

There was the story I heard later, of the instructor who had a favorite trick with students having difficulty learning to land. After exhausting the usual means, above the traffic pattern somewhere he would shake the control stick from side to side, banging the student's knees—the front and rear sticks were connected—to get his attention. He would then remove the pin holding the rear stick in place and, with the student twisting his neck to see what was happening, wave it in the air and toss it over the side, pointing at the student with the gesture *You, you've got it*, and pointing down. It had always worked. One day for still another lagging student he rattled the stick fiercely, flourished it, and tossed it away. The student nodded numbly, bent down, unfastened his own stick, and ignoring the instructor's cries, threw it away also. He watched as the frightened instructor bailed out and then, fame assured, reached down for the spare stick he had secretly brought along, flew back to the field, and landed.

∽

To solve the complexities of the traffic pattern, I had made, for quick reference, a small card with a diagram of each of the possible patterns on it. Entry was always at forty-five degrees to a downwind leg, but to work it all out backwards and head straight for the proper point was confusing, and nothing seemed to annoy York as much as starting to turn the wrong way. The worst was when the wind changed while you were away from the field; the pattern had shifted, and everything you had tried to remember was useless.

A week passed thus. We fly to an auxiliary field, a large meadow five or ten minutes away. There is bare earth near the borders where planes have repeatedly touched down.

"Let's try some landings," he says. Nervously I go over in my mind what to do, what not. "Make three good ones and I'll get out."

We come in for the first. "Hold that airspeed," he directs. "That's good. Now come back on the power. Start rounding out."

Somehow it works. Hardly a bump as the wheels touch. "Good." I push the throttle forward in a smooth motion and we are off again.

The second landing is the same. I am not certain what I have done but whatever it is, I try to repeat it for the third.

Almost confidently I turn onto final once more. "You're doing fine," he says. I watch the airspeed as we descend. The grass field is approaching, the decisive third.

"Make this a full stop," he instructs. I ease back the throttle. The airspeed begins to drop. "Keep the nose down," he suddenly warns. "Nose down! Watch your airspeed!" I feel a hand on the stick. The plane is beginning to tremble. Untouched by me the throttle leaps forward, but through it somehow we are falling, unsupported by the roar. With a huge jolt we hit the ground, bounce, and come down again. He utters a single contemptuous word. When we have slowed, he says, "Taxi over there, to the left." I follow his instructions. We come to a stop.

"That was terrible. You rounded out twenty feet in the air. As far as I can make out, you're going to kill us both." I see him rising up. He climbs out of the cockpit and stands on the wing. "You take her up," he says.

This consent, the words of which I could not even imagine. Alone in the plane, I do what we had done each time, taxi to the end of the bare spot, turn, and almost mechanically advance the throttle. I felt at that moment—I will remember always—the thrill of the inachievable. Reciting to myself, exuberant, immortal, I felt the plane leave the ground and cross the hayfields and farms, making a noise like a tremendous, bumbling fly. I was far out, beyond the reef, nervous but unfrightened, knowing nothing, certain of all, cloth helmet, childish face, sleeve wind-maddened as I held an ecstatic arm out in the slipstream, the exaltation, the godliness, at last!

∽

At night in the white wooden barracks not far from the flight line we talked of flying, in the clamor of the student mess, and on the battered busses swaying into town. We walked the streets in aimless groups, past lawyers' offices with names painted in gold on the windows. There were tracks through the center of Pine Bluff along which freight trains moved with provincial slowness. There was the gold-domed courthouse and the bulky Pines Hotel, even then middle-aged with a portico entrance, balconies, and mysterious rooms. Of the silent residential neighborhoods with large clapboard houses or lesser ones set on the bare ground, we know nothing. From the desolate life of the town on many Sundays we returned willingly to the field.

∽

We flew less often with the instructor. It was late spring, the sky fresh and filled with fair-weather clouds—weather, which could mean so much, was already a preoccupation. Late in the day the clouds would become dense and towering, their edges struck with light; epic clouds, the last of the sun streaming through.

One afternoon, alone, I caught sight in their tops, far above, of a B-24 moving along like a great liner. Dazzled by its distance and height I turned like a dinghy to follow until it was gone.

∽

At noon they were talking about someone's extraordinary grade, one of the regular air cadets with whom we were train-

Pine Bluff, spring 1944

ing. His score had been six. It seemed unbelievable. He was pointed out—suddenly everyone knew who he was—the one with the dark hair. I could see him in the food line, distinct from the others, slim, at ease. He had flown before, it turned out. He already had a pilot's license and sixty hours in a Cub.

The hurdles in primary were soloing and then two check rides with an Air Force pilot given, I believe, after forty and sixty hours of flying time. Don't forget to salute before and after the flight, they said, and be sure you can explain the maintenance form. In the air there would be brief commands to do this or that maneuver and at some inconvenient moment the throttle would be pulled back with the announcement, "Forced landing."

The shakiest students confessed their fears and often did worse because of them, but some failures were unforeseeable, even unimaginable, like that of the dark-haired angel who had scored the six. One day he disappeared. He had somehow failed his forty-hour check and was gone. It made you realize how flimsy your position was and how unforgiving the machinery behind it all. The least promising of us, though we did not know it then, those with the least élan, would go to bombers and attack aircraft, and the others to fighters. That was a year off. Meanwhile, one by one they were dropping away, sometimes the leaders.

∽

In early 1945, the final battles in both Europe and the Pacific were being fought. Salter's class was finishing flight training and was to graduate at the beginning of June.

༚

We were gone all spring and summer and returned much changed. We marched less perfectly, dressed with less care. West Point, its officer's sashes and cock feathers fluttering from the shakos, its stewardship, somehow passed over to those who had stayed.

Among the firsts: first solo, first breath of outside air, in here belongs first love affair . . .

There was, that year, a then-irresistible novel called *Shore Leave* with a pair of Navy wings on its blue jacket, and written in a confident style. It became, at my insistence, our text. The name of its nihilist hero, gaunt and faithless, was Crewson. He had flown at Midway and in other battles. The blood baths. Would he remember as an old man, the author, Frederic Wakeman, wrote, rising at three in the morning on the third of June? The briefing at four and soon afterwards reports of enemy aircraft inbound. And then on the dense rippled sea, *the Kaga, steaming upwind at a brisk thirty knots, the coming-out-of-the-ether feeling when he split his flaps and made an eighty-degree dive for the red circle on her flight deck . . . the first hit . . .* —all this was indelible. Those bombs going home freed him forever from the trivial and mundane.

His society girlfriend was only one of the women who trotted after him like colts.

We shared this book as a Bible might be shared by a devout couple. It was a hymn to the illicit. Emboldened by it we acted as though we were part of the war. On the inside cover she inscribed it to me, the Crewson of her past. There were many things in it that she could have written herself, she continued, and then, as if granting to a beloved child possession of a favorite plaything, *Keep this book with you, my dearest.* If things had turned out differently, it managed to say, if we had, in the way of all failed lovers, only met years sooner or later . . .

෩

At Stewart Field the final spring, nearly pilots, we had the last segment of training. This was near Newburgh, about forty minutes from West Point. We wore flying suits most of the day and lived in long, open-bay barracks. That photograph of oneself, nonexistent, that no one ever sees, in my case was taken in the morning by the doorway of what must be the day-room and I am drinking a Coke from an icy, greenish bottle, a ritual prelude to all the breakfastless mornings of flying that were to come. During all the training there had been few fatalities. We were that good. At least I knew I was.

On a May evening after supper we took off, one by one, on a navigation flight. It was still daylight and the planes, as they departed were soon lost in their solitude. On the maps the course was drawn, miles marked off in ticks of ten. The route lay to the west, over the wedged-up Allegheny ridges to Port Jervis and Scranton, then down to Reading, and the last long leg of the triangle back home. It was all mechanical with one exception: the winds aloft had been incorrectly forecast. Unknown to us, they were from a different direction and stronger. Alone and confident we headed west.

The air at altitude has a different smell, metallic and faintly tinged with gasoline or exhaust. The ground floats by with tidal slowness, the roads desolate, the rivers unmoving. It is exactly like the map, with certain insignificant differences which one ponders over but leaves unresolved.

The sun has turned red and sunk lower. The airspeed reads one-sixty. The fifteen or twenty airplanes, invisible to one another, are in a long, irregular string. Behind, the sky has become a deeper shade. The color of the earth was muted and the towns seemed empty shadows. There was no one to see or talk to. The wind, unsuspected, was shifting us slowly, like sand.

On my mind apart from navigation were, I suppose, New York nights, the lure of the city, various achievements that a year or two before I had only dreamed of. The first dim star appeared and then, somewhat to the left of where it should be, the drab scrawl of Scranton.

Flying, like most things of consequence, is method. Though I did not know it then, I was behaving improperly. There were light-lines between cities in those days, like lights on an unseen highway but much farther apart. By reading their flashed codes you could tell where you were, but I was not bothering with that. I turned south towards Reading. The sky was dark now. Far below, the earth was cooling, giving up the heat of the day. A mist had begun to form. In it the light-lines would fade away and also, almost shyly, the towns. I flew on.

It is a different world at night. The instruments become harder to read, details disappear from the map. After a while I tuned to the Reading frequency and managed to pick up its signal. I had no radio compass but there was a way of determining, by flying a certain sequence of headings, where in a surrounding quadrant you were. Then if the signal slowly increased in strength you were inbound towards the station. If not, and you had to turn up the volume to continue hearing it, you were going away. It was primitive but it worked.

When the time came I waited to see if I had passed or was still approaching Reading. The minutes went by. At first I couldn't detect a change but then the signal seemed to grow weaker. I turned north and flew, watching the clock. Something was wrong, something serious: the signal didn't change. I was lost, not only literally but in relation to reality. Meanwhile the wind, unseen, fateful, was forcing me farther north.

Among the stars, one was moving. It was the lights of another plane, perhaps one from the squadron. In any case, wherever it was headed there would be a field. I pushed up the throttle. As I drew closer, on an angle, I began to make out what it was, an airliner, a DC-3. It might be going to St. Louis or Chicago. I had already been flying for what seemed like hours and had begun, weakhearted, a repeated checking of fuel. The gauges were on the floor, one on each side of the seat. I tried not to think of them but they were like a wound; I could not keep myself from glancing down.

Slowly the airliner and its lights became more distant. I couldn't keep up with it. I turned northeast, the general direction of home. I had been scribbling illegibly on the page of memory, which way I had gone and for how long. I now had no idea where I was. The occasional lights on the ground of unknown towns, lights blurred and yellowish, meant nothing. Allentown, which should have been somewhere, never appeared. There was a terrible temptation to abandon everything, to give up, as with a hopeless puzzle. I was reciting "Invictus" to myself, *I am the master of my fate* . . . It availed nothing. I had the greatest difficulty not praying and finally I did, flying in the noisy darkness, desperate for the sight of a city or anything that would give me my position.

In the map case of the airplane was a booklet, *What to Do If Lost*, and suddenly remembering, I got it out and with my flashlight began to read. There was a list of half a dozen steps to take in order. My eye skidded down it. The first ones I had already tried. Others, like tuning in any radio range and orienting yourself on it, I had given up on, something was wrong with that, it wasn't working. I managed to get the signal from Stewart Field but didn't take up the prescribed heading. I could tell from its faintness—it was indistinct in a thicket of other sounds—that I was far away, and I had lost faith in the procedure. The final advice seemed more practical. If you think you are to the west of Stewart, it said, head east until you come to the Hudson River and then fly north or south; you will eventually come to New York or Albany.

It was past eleven, the sky dense with stars, the earth a void. I had turned east. The dimly lit fuel gauges read twenty-five gallons or so in each wing. The idea slowly growing, of opening the canopy and struggling into the wind, over the side into blackness, tumbling, parachuting down, was not as unthinkable as that of giving the airplane itself up to destruction. I would be washed out, I knew. The anguish was unbearable. I had been flying east for ten minutes but it seemed hours. Occasionally I made out the paltry lights of some small town or group of houses, barely distinguishable, but otherwise nothing. The cities had vanished, sunken to darkness. I looked down again. Twenty gallons.

Suddenly off to the left there was a glimmer that became—I

was just able to make it out—a faint string of lights and then slowly, magically, two parallel lines. It was the bridge at Poughkeepsie. Dazed with relief I tried to pick out its dark lines and those of the river, turning to keep it in sight, going lower and lower. Then, in the way that all things certain had changed that night, the bridge changed too. At about a thousand feet above them, stricken, I saw I was looking at the streetlights of some town.

The gauges read fifteen gallons. One thing that should never be done—it had been repeated to us often—was to attempt a forced landing at night. But I had no choice. I began to circle, able in the mist to see clearly only what was just beneath. The town was at the edge of some hills; I banked away from them in the blackness. If I went too far from the brightly lit, abandoned main street, I lost my bearings. Dropping even lower I saw dark roofs everywhere and amid them, unexpectedly, a blank area like a lake or small park. I had passed it quickly, turned, and lost it. Finally, lower still, I saw it again. It was not big but there was nothing else. I ducked my head for a moment to look down—the number beneath each index line was wavering slightly: ten gallons, perhaps twelve.

The rule for any strange field was to first fly across at minimum altitude to examine the surface. I was not even sure it was a field; it might be water or a patch of woods. If a park, it might have buildings or fences. I turned onto a downwind leg or what I judged to be one, then a base leg, letting down over swiftly enlarging roofs. I had the canopy open to cut reflection, the ghostly duplication of instruments, the red warning lights. I stared ahead through the wind and noise. I was at a hundred feet or so, flaps down, still descending.

In front, coming fast, was my field. In a panel near my knee were the landing light switches with balled tips to make them identifiable by feel. I reached for them blindly. The instant they came on I knew I'd made a mistake. They blazed like searchlights in the mist; I could see more without them but the ground was twenty feet beneath me, I was at minimum speed and dared not bend to turn them off. Something went by on the left. Trees, in the middle of the park. I had barely missed them. No landing here. A moment later, at the far end, more trees. They were higher than I was, and without speed to climb I banked to get through them. I heard foliage slap the wings as just ahead, shielded, a second rank of trees rose up. There was no time to do anything. Something large struck a wing. It tore away. The plane careened up. It stood poised for an endless moment, one landing light flooding a house into which an instant later it crashed.

Nothing has vanished, not even the stunned first seconds of silence, the torn leaves drifting down. Reflexively, as a slain man might bewilderedly shut a door, I reached to turn off the ignition. I was badly injured, though in what way I did not know. There was no pain. My legs, I realized. I tried to move them. Nothing seemed wrong. My front teeth were loose; I could feel them move as I breathed. In absolute quiet I sat for a few moments almost at a loss as to what to do, then unbuckled the harness and stepped from the cockpit onto what had been the front porch. The nose of the plane was in the wreckage of a room. The severed wing lay back in the street.

The house, as it turned out, belonged to a family that was welcoming home a son who had been a prisoner of war in Germany. They were having a party and had taken the startling noise of the plane as it passed low over town many times to be some sort of military salute, and though it was nearly midnight had all gone into the street to have a look. I had come in like a meteorite over their heads. The town was Great Barrington. I had to be shown where it was on a map, in Massachusetts, miles to the north and east . . .

◦◦

They came for me the next day and I watched them load the wreckage on a large flatbed truck. I rode back with the remains of the plane. In the barracks, which were empty when I arrived, my bed, unlike the rows of others, was littered with messages, all mock congratulations. I found myself, unexpectedly, a popular figure. It was as if I had somehow defied the authorities. On the blackboard in the briefing room was a

Great Barrington: The Graham house, May 8, 1945

drawing of a house with the tail of an airplane sticking from the roof and written beneath, *Geisler's student.* I survived the obligatory check-rides and proceedings of the accident board, which were brief.

∽

> *From the end of the war, Salter spent six years, 1945-1951, stationed in the Pacific and back in the States, typical of a career officer. He was in a transport squadron for about a year and afterwards occasionally flew a fighter.*

∽

In the Pacific the war had ended but its vast, shabby landscape remained. In Manila Bay the water was the color of rust from sunken ships. Unidentified masts and funnels were sticking above the surface. Manila was half destroyed; the tops were blown off the palm trees, the roads were ruined, the air filled with dust. There were still rotting helmets and field equipment to be found on Bataan. The licit had disappeared. Theft was an industry, deserters coming into barracks before dawn to steal what they could. There were incomplete rosters, slack discipline. Men were threatening to shoot officers who were too conscientious. On Okinawa a corporal was driving a nurse around to the black units in an unmarked ambulance. She lay on a bed in back, naked from the waist down. She charged twenty dollars . . .

We were at last sent to squadrons where a few languid old-timers reigned, secure figures who were on intimate terms with the supply sergeant and knew how everything was done. The fighter pilots went to remote fields in Korea, Japan, Okinawa. With fifteen or twenty others I was sent to transports and stayed on for a while in Manila, living in corrugated-iron huts that the last of the wartime flyers had abandoned, leaving behind among other things amateur photos of nude Australian girls and addresses scribbled in pencil on the back of instrument cards.

It was not long before, like the onset of a disease, the win-

nowing began. Word of mouth brought the news—someone
had seen someone, someone had heard . . . Men began to disappear. One by one there came the names.

Did you hear about McGranery? they said. Spun in on
Palawan in a P-51. Gassman was killed there, too. Jack Ray,
always smiling, was killed on Okinawa. Woods crashed in a
coral pit on takeoff there and died. The planes had to be flown
correctly or they were treacherous; they would stall, one wing
dropping abruptly, like a horse stumbling. At low speed, on a
go-around, suddenly opening the throttle could make them
roll onto their back, the controls unable to prevent it.

Schrader was dead, we heard. MacDonald. Like drops of
pelting rain they were exploding in the dust. Averill got killed
in Korea, going around in a P-38. Domey was killed; Joe
Macur. Cherry got killed; Jim Smart, the streamers curling
from his wingtips as he went into the sea.

The accidents. They were the stark trees in the forest that
stood alone, at the foot of which nothing thereafter grew. The
wreckage of the cities would be cleared away but never the oil
slick on the sea that was all they found of Smart. For me, however, it was a siren song—the fierce metal planes with their
weathered insignia, the great noise as they launched, the distant runways at Negros, Yontan, Cebu. The danger of it was a
distinction which nothing else could afford. It would not happen to you, of course, it would never happen to you, and also,

as has been pointed out, you could discover death as quickly by fleeing from it, be stung the soonest...

Who had been killed—it was that for years. I flew in many funeral formations. Timed to pass over the chapel as the officers and wives, the widow among them, emerged, two flights of four, tight as nails, roaring past with one ship conspicuously missing. In the evening the piano is playing at the club. They are rolling dice at the bar. You are surviving, more than surviving: their days have been inscribed on yours.

∽

You remember the airfields, the first sight of some, the deep familiarity of others... I liked fields near the sea, Westhampton Beach on Long Island, Myrtle Beach, Langley, Elgin, Alameda, where we landed in the fall, ferrying planes to be shipped to the fighting in Korea... There are fields I would like to forget, Polk, where one night, as a rank amateur, I nearly went into the trees, trying clumsily to go around with my flaps down. Later, in the wooden barracks, came another lesson. Two men in flying suits, drab in appearance paused at the open door of the room where I sat on the bed. "Are you the one flying the P-51? Where are you from?" one asked.

"Andrews," I said. I felt a kind of glamour, being connected with the silvery plane and its slim, aggressive shape, parked by itself on the ramp. It was not hard to deduce that they were lesser figures, transport pilots probably. I told them I was in the Fourth Group rather than going into the less interesting facts—I was actually a graduate student at Georgetown. They did not seem very impressed. "Ever hear of Don Garland?" I said, naming a noted pilot in the Fourth.

"Who's that?"

"One of the best pilots in the Air Force."

"Oh, yeah?"

I offered a few exaggerations I had overheard at one time or another in the Andrews Club. Garland flew the slot position on the acrobatic team, hanging there with his bare teeth, so to speak, the proof of it being the blackened rudder of his ship, stained by the leader's exhaust and as a mark of pride always left that way—no mechanic would dare rub it clean. He was a wild man, Garland—I could tell them any number of stories.

"What does he look like?"

I gave a vague answer. Was he a decent guy? they wanted to know.

I had almost been in a fight one evening at Andrews, not with Garland but with another member of the team. "Not particularly," I said.

Suddenly one of them began laughing. The other glanced at him. "Shut up," he said.

"Oh, for Christ's sake," the first one said. Then to me, "This is Garland," he said, gesturing.

I was speechless.

"What the hell's your name?" they wanted to know.

I left early in the morning, before they were up.

∽

Late in the summer of 1951 I entered at last the realm long sought and was sent to Presque Isle, Maine, to the 75th Fighter Squadron.

∽

In November, in northern Maine, you might see two of them from far off, at the end of the runway set amid the fields. They are barely identifiable, early F-86s with thin, swept wings. Nearer there is the sound, wavering but full, like a distant cataract. Then, close, it becomes a roar with the smoke billowing up behind. They are being run up, engines full open, brakes on, needles trembling at their utmost.

The pilot of the first airplane has his head bent forward over the instruments as if examining them closely. Red-haired, gaunt, he had so far said almost nothing to me. His name was Stewart. I knew little about him. He was a Korean veteran and a maintenance officer. Lined up beside him, I waited. Why do you remember some things above all others and men who have hardly spoken a word to you? I was new in the group and nervous. I was determined to fly good formation, to be a shadow, almost touching him. We were taking off just before sunset. No one else would be flying.

His head rose then and turned towards me. His hand came up and hesitated. I nodded. The hand dropped.

Wreathed in thunder we started down the runway. Gathering speed I saw his arm suddenly swinging wildly in a circle. I had no idea what it meant, was I to go on, was he aborting? In a moment I saw it was neither, only exhilaration; he was waving us onward as if whipping a bandana around in the air. The noses came up; we were at liftoff speed. I saw the ground fall away and from that moment for him I ceased to be.

There was a low overcast through which we shot, and above it brilliant reddening sky. I was barely twenty feet from him but he never so much as glanced at me. He sat in the cockpit like a prophet, alone and in thought, head turning unhurriedly from side to side. We had reached thirty thousand feet when the tower called. Weather was moving in, our mission had been canceled. "Operations advises you return to base," they said.

"Roger," I heard him say matter-of-factly. "We'll be in after a few minutes. We're going to burn out some petrol."

With that he rolled over and, power on, headed straight down. I didn't know what he intended or was even doing. I fell into close trail, hanging there grimly as if he were watching. The airspeed went to the red line; thousands of feet were spinning off the altimeter. The controls grew stiff, the stick could be moved only with great effort as we went through rolls and steep turns at speeds so great I could feel my heart being forced down from my chest.

We burst through the overcast and into the narrow strip of sky beneath. I'd moved to his wing again. We were well over five hundred knots at about fifteen hundred feet. It was almost impossible to stay in position in the turns. I had both hands on the stick. All the time we were dropping lower. We were not moving, it seemed. We were fixed, quivering, fatally close.

Five hundred feet, three hundred, still lower, in what seemed deathly silence except for an incandescent, steady roar, in solitude, slamming every moment against invisible waves of air. He was leading us into the unknown. My flying suit was soaked, the sweat ran down my face. A pure pale halo formed in back of his canopy and remained there, streaming like smoke. I began to realize what it was about. Never looking at me, absorbed by the instruments in front of him and by something in his thoughts, sometimes watching the world of dark forest that swept beneath us, hills and frozen lakes, he was gauging my desire to belong. It was a baptism. This silent angel was to bring me to the place where, wet and subdued, I would be made one with the rest. If, like a scrap of paper held out the window of a speeding train, my airplane were to instantly come apart, torn bits tumbling and fluttering behind, he would only have begun a large, unhasty turn to see what had happened, his expression unchanged.

I had surrendered myself to all of it and to whatever might come when unexpectedly he turned towards the field. We had already crossed it two or three times. This time we entered on initial approach and dropped dive brakes, slowing as we turned. I had a feeling of absolute control of the airplane. It was tamed, obedient. I could have gently tapped his wing with mine, I felt, and not left a dent. I could have followed him anywhere, through anything.

I remember that moment and the smoothness of landing in the fading light. Now that the sound of our passing violently overhead had disappeared, on the field all was still. There was unbroken calm. Our idling engines had a high-pitched, lonely whine.

Afterwards he said not a word to me. The emissary does not stoop to banter. He performs his duty, gathers his things, and is gone. But the snowy fields pouring past beneath us, the terror, the feeling of being for a moment a true pilot—these things remained.

∽

Friends on the outside were always asking why he stayed in, or telling him he was wasting himself. He had never been able to give an answer. With the fresh shirt on his shoulders still cold as ice, chilled from an hour in an unheated radar compartment

Presque Isle, fall of 1951

at forty thousand feet . . . the marks from the oxygen mask still on his face, and on his hands the microscopic grit of a thousand-mile journey, he had tried to find an answer sitting alone at dinner in the club filled with administrative majors and mothers talking about their children, but he never could. In his mind he carried Saturdays of flying, with the autumnal roar of crowds on the radio compass and the important stadiums thirty minutes apart and button-small, the wingmen like metallic arrows poised in the air above a continent, the last sunlight slanting through the ground haze, and cities of concrete moss; but never any reasonable reply. Or, sick of the stars and bored with speed on those nights in the great black sea, the surf of which was cities bubbling on the wave, listening to the others who were up, two unseen killers perhaps, calling themselves Butcher Red and seeking themselves in the darkness, he had tried to think of one—brief, understandable—but never could. It was a secret life, lived alone.

∽

I felt I was born for it. One of the initial things I did when I went up without a chase plane in an F-86 was climb to altitude and shut the engine off. The sky was suddenly flooded with silence, the metal deadweight. Calmly, though my fingers were tingling, I went through the steps to restart it, air start, it was called. Afterwards I did it again. I wanted to be confident of the procedure in case of a flame-out, and following that I never thought of them with dread.

The true hierarchy was based on who was the best pilot and who flew the most. There might be an obvious leader or two or three near equals. One quickly sensed who they were. In addition there were those who had flown in combat. Their stories were listened to more attentively. There was a big, overconfident pilot in another squadron who starred in one of the first I heard. He had flown F-80s, the earliest jet, in Korea. He was coming back from a mission one day, leading his flight home, at thirty thousand feet on top of an overcast. He called radar for a vector, "Milkman, this is Maple Lead."

Milkman answered, identified the flight on the radar screen, and gave them heading and distance to their field, which was K-2: One hundred and seventy degrees and a hundred and twenty miles.

The flight was low on fuel and the weather deteriorating. They would have to make an instrument approach, the leader knew. He called his element leader for a fuel check, "What state, Three?"

The fuel gauge on the F-80 had a small window where the pilot set in the number of gallons he had at takeoff, and thereafter, like an odometer in reverse, they clicked off during the flight. "Sixty gallons, Lead," the element leader replied.

"No sweat."

The clouds were solid. They could see nothing. After a while the radar station gave them another steer, still one hundred and seventy degrees, ninety-five miles.

"How are you doing, Three?"

"Forty-two gallons."

"Roger."

The ships, not far apart, could do nothing to affect one another though they shared a common fate. There was no need to speak. Silent minutes passed. The gallons fell away.

"Milkman, Maple Lead. Where do you have us now?"

"Stand by one, Maple Lead. We have you . . . steer one eight zero to home plate, sixty-six nautical miles."

"Roger. Sixty-six out. Will you inform K-2 that we're in the soup, low on fuel? We'll be declaring an emergency." Then, to the element leader, "What do you have, Three?"

"Twenty-four gallons."

That was six or seven minutes of flying at altitude, throttled back to minimum cruise, but they also had to let down, make an approach, line up with the runway if they could find it. The heads in the cockpits were motionless, as if nothing of interest were going on, but they were facing the unalterable. The wingmen might have even less fuel than the element leader. After a while the flight leader called again, "Milkman, Maple. How far are we out?"

"We have you thirty-four miles out, Maple flight."

"Roger." He looked over at the element leader, who was perhaps fifty feet away. "What do you have now, Brax?"

"I've got nine hundred ninety-eight gallons, buddy," the reply came calmly.

Not long afterwards, one by one, they ran out of fuel. The entire flight dead-sticked onto the runway at K-2.

It was among the knowledgeable others that one hoped to be talked about and admired. It was not impossible—the world of squadrons is small. The years would bow to you; you would be remembered, your name like a thoroughbred's, a horse that ran and won.

∽

My closet friend in the squadron, a classmate, had hair flecked with gray and a wry way of talking that I liked. William Wood was his name. He was older—he'd been perhaps twenty when we became cadets, and afterwards had gone right into fighters; he'd been in them since the beginning. He was relaxed and could be very droll.

Early that winter, he and I went to Korea. We had eagerly read—it passed from hand to hand—the first definitive report, a sort of letter about the enemy airplanes that had suddenly appeared in the war, Russian planes, MIG-15s, and when the chance came, like men running to a claims office, we had raced to volunteer. There were two openings that month and we got them. It was not only the report, the war itself was whispering an invitation: Meet me. Whatever we were, we felt inauthentic. You were not anything unless you had fought.

II.

The Korean War began suddenly in June 1950 when North Korea attacked the South across a line that had divided the country—much as East and West Germany had been divided—since the end of the Second World War in 1945. North Korea was in the Communist sphere. The South was relatively democratic and free.

General MacArthur, who had been presiding over the American occupation of Japan nearby, brilliantly constructed victory from what seemed disaster in Korea and swept the Communist forces back to the northern limit of the country where the Yalu River serves to separate it from China. Then, in a surprise move the Chinese, labeling their forces "volunteers," crossed the Yalu in overwhelming numbers and drove the American and South Korean armies back to nearly the original line of demarcation where the war settled into a bloody stalemate.

There was heavy fighting in the air. Large numbers of the latest Soviet fighter, the MIG-15, flown for the most part by Russian pilots, challenged American control of the air. For American fighter pilots in Korea, the tour was 100 combat missions.

∽

2 Feb 1952. Pittsburgh, en route. Los Medanos, one of those bars with a long mirror and nymphs etched on it. Officers and cheap-looking women. The Belgian hatcheck girl, stunning figure.

—I don't think your friend is feeling very well, she said to Woody.

—Oh, he's just puking, Woody said.

The hotel was in a square like a Spanish courthouse. Rooms by the hour.

∽

4 Feb 1952. I called Ann from Travis before we left. It was affectionate but stiff. Perhaps my fault as much as hers. Perhaps she wasn't alone.

Hickam Field. I hardly remembered it. The warm air, mynah birds calling as we sat in the terminal, debriefing and filling out white cards. The wooden BOQs along Worthington, depressing as ever. I remembered coming into their emptiness on afternoons when work ended.

Sitting in Wahine Kapu with Woody. Many nights here or on the lanai with its smooth dance floor, card games in the nipa huts all night long, dinner parties.

Flying out again, over the brilliance of the beaches, the dark sea. The vibration flows through the airplane from the engines, playing every loose piece of metal. Hour after hour over the water, the sound of the engines seeming to rise and fall like the breath of a sick man through a critical night.

This endless struggle against the miles. The plane doesn't move evenly, but with little lurches against the uneven air. All along the fuselage, like an orchestra of metal insects, the loose pieces take up the tune.

6 Feb 1952. Tokyo. Snow. The Pearl House Hotel on Avenue B, three stories squeezed in between little shops. One bathroom, just off the lobby. Bar filled with GIs. In the room, dim bulbs, a gas burner for heat. Two pairs of slippers beneath the bed, one large, one small.

The cab finally comes. Miyoshi's. Dark night, remote neighborhood. Short path to the door. We've been drinking. In stocking feet led to a room along a corridor. Whiskey is brought. A few minutes later, a tapping on the door. Two girls enter, bowing. One has a samisen, plays and sings in a high voice. In kimonos we go to the baths, sit naked on wooden stools, the girls soaping us, Mitsiko and Hanako. Hard-ons like horses'. All naked together in the water. Then they dry us.

—You rear gentermen.

—We're no gentlemen.

—Yes, yes. You are.

—No.

—You good captains, she insists.

—No, no good.

—No-good captains?

Sex on tatami mats. Smooth belly, little pubic hair.

In the baths the next morning at seven, sitting on the warm floor, shaving. Soaking in the hot water. Cold, gray skies, smokestacks and black buildings. Singing *You Must Have Been a Beautiful Baby.*

Cab comes at exactly 0900. Drive to the station. The bill at Miyoshi's was 5,000 yen each.

Train to Nagoya and Iwakuni. Leaves on the dot. The country is green and clear all the way from Tokyo to Nagoya. Orange trees, tea bushes, rice stubble in the fields. We follow the sea as far as Atami skirting little fishing villages. Stations with concrete platforms, vendors selling oranges, candy, beer. At ten that night we change to a troop sleeper, arrive at Iwakuni at six in the morning. Dark, cold, clean-smelling air. Remembering coming back to West Point by boat after the Columbia or Notre Dame game, walking up the steep hill to the Plain at this hour.

By truck through town. Lighted, empty streets. Across river on bomb-damaged bridge to air base. Sound of an airplane taking off. Dawn just breaking, buildings turning from black to gray. Sunday morning, all still.

12 Feb 1952. Korea. A bus came to take us to Kimpo from Seoul City. Drove along outskirts. Everything dirty and poor, cracked walls, rusted iron, grass roofs on many houses crowded close, streets unpaved. Ragged kids begging from soldiers. River frozen, trees bare. A few old men had chopped holes in the ice to fish.

Watched a mission take off at K-14—two at a time, booming down the runway, then two more, and two more. Col. Thyng was leading, north to the Yalu. A second squadron followed. They streamed out, turning, disappearing into the overcast.

Come now, and let us go and risk our lives unnecessarily. For if they have got any value at all it is this that they have got none. We arrived in Korea, as it happened, on a gloomy day. It was February, the dead of winter, planes parked among sandbag revetments and bitter cold lying over the field adding to the pall. Davis, the ranking American ace—mythic word, ineffaceable—a squadron commander, had just been shot down. With the terrible mark of newness on us, we stood in the officers' club and listened to what was or was not fact. We were too fresh to make distinctions.

F-86s taking off for a mission, Korean War

Davis was CO of the 334th Squadron. He had twelve kills. He was leading B Flight. Col. Preston, the Group CO, was leading the squadron. Near the Yalu, Davis dove on 15 MIGs that were in a climb, got the leader and swung out to try to get another. He did but was hit with a 37mm just behind the canopy before his wingman could call a break. He went down in a slow turn, hit and burned.

The flags on the field were at half-mast. At the club they were talking about MIGs, how good they were, how much better than the 86 at altitude. Chuck Pratt had been shot down, we heard.

Walking back to quarters in the rain. Wet road, dark, cold.

—I'm not going to like it here, Woody muttered.

∽

We had come, it turned out, to join a sort of crude colonial life lived in stucco buildings in plain, square rooms, unadorned, with common showers and a latrine that even the wing commander shared.

We were there together for six months, cold winter mornings with the weak sunlight on the hills, the silvery airplanes gliding forth like mechanical serpents not quite perfected in their movement and then forming on the runway amid rising sound. In the spring the ice melted in the rivers and the willow

Woody

became green. The blood from a bloody nose poured down over your mouth and chin inside the rubber oxygen mask. In summer the locust trees were green and all the fields. It comes hauntingly back: silent, unknown lands; distant brown river, the Yalu, the line between two worlds.

∽

Just as, they say, in North Africa during the war the thing to have immediately to hide your innocence was desert boots, so the first requirement of a pilot in Korea was a folding plastic-covered map of the long peninsula that projected down from China into the Yellow Sea, the muddy Yalu its northern border, the spattering of numerous islands, and midway, the enemy capital, Pyongyang. Over the area of North Korea we drew a fan of lines, all converging on our base. This gave headings, especially to home. Arcs of distance crossed these vectors to show at a glance how far you had gone or had to go.

From the front lines, which crossed the country at the waist, it was about two hundred miles, twenty-five minutes or so, to the river and only a few more to the enemy fields in China, where we were forbidden to go. There was no struggle for possession of the air. Like a backroom deal, that had already been decided. The MIGs entered the sky over North Korea at will, fought if they chose to, and went back to their fields. We were trying to exterminate the enemy, but even the

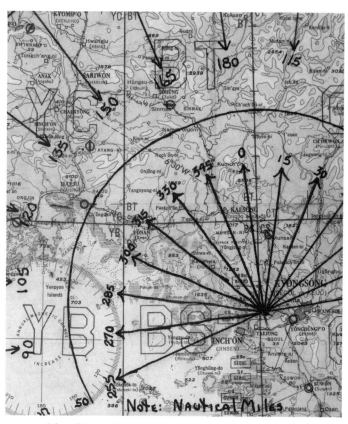

Detail from fighter pilot's map of North Korea, the azimuth lines radiate from K-14, the home base, north to the Yalu River 200 miles away.

boy who mows the lawn knows that you do not kill wasps one
by one, you destroy the nest. The nests, however, were not to
be touched. Everything in between was contested.

༒

20 Feb 1952. Early morning. Through the dirty window the sky
pale blue with cirrus. Alarm clocks haven't gone off. The P-51
reccy's are on the runway, blasting their engines. They're first
off every morning. The RF-80s come later. The end of the
runway is only about three hundred yards away. Sparrows scur-
rying beneath the eaves giving their brittle calls.

Shaving in a pan of hot water that's been on the stove all

Flight line at K-14: Planes are in sandbag revetments

night, the water steaming as it hits the cold earth outside the door. Cracked mirror. Mess hall down the icy road. Shirt, sweater, flight jacket. Air very cold, in it become instantly awake.

∽

The first mission was taxiing out. The ships, some painted with black-and-white zebra stripes, others with a solid band of yellow, moved along quickly, but they seemed strangely inept on the ground, rolling like cable cars or trolleys. A few of them had red stars stenciled under the cockpit rim. He saw the pilots hunched inside, faceless and inhuman under the helmets and black oxygen masks.

They lined up in pairs on the runway, twelve ships altogether. The engines were run up. The smoke shot backward and skyward. A sustained roar filled the air, a deafening eruption, like an ultimate wind of flame. The noise was brutal, but deep and assuring. It seemed endless. The rear ships quivered in the river of blast. He watched the first two finally go, their rudders flicking slowly from side to side as they began to roll, like the tails of fish holding quietly against a current, rolling very slowly at the start and then quickening until they flowed down the far end of the runway and nosed into the sky. The others followed at close interval.

∽

23 Feb 1952. First combat mission. Sightseeing tour, up to Long Dong, across the peninsula to Wonson, then home. Cold, damp day. Bitter wind. Bones feeling brittle, nose running.

Somewhat nervous. Supposed to be Purple Two, the last man, on MacDonald's wing. Somehow mistook Griffith's plane for MacDonald's and taxied out in wrong flight. Never got it straightened out. Difficult to tell earth from sea. The frozen river mouths blended into the land. The sky clear and ominous. A few contrails. Passed head-on a returning squadron of 86s. Frost forming on rear of canopy at 41,000 feet despite canopy heat. Rearview mirror missing. Spent time looking hard but not really focusing. Felt stuffed into cockpit, loaded with layers of clothing and equipment. The last ninety-nine missions, they say, are the hardest.

Squadron party that night at the enlisted mess. Walls used as a blackboard for an English-Japanese course, grammar chalked all over them. A band, steaks, beer, everyone shouldering one another in the smoke, shouting and singing. Col. Thyng and Col. Preston, dutifully there, sitting quietly at one table.

∽

The first morning light over the top of the wing. The first, easy missions. Out of the dust of memory, with a faint coating of dust himself, childlike, shrewd, comes Amell, the squadron commander ... I don't remember how I first saw him. He remains fixed, in any event, as in a photograph, with a fur hat like a Cossack and a navy revolver in a holster under his arm. He had a husky, somewhat thespian voice. As an actor his speeches tended to be slightly long, although he could be succinct on occasion ... His eyes were bad. They used to say that if anyone had the chances Amell had, they would have shot down ten airplanes—he ended up with three victories and a wingman drenched in flame who went down one day near Sinuiju. As I think now of his eyes, they seem to me small but like those of traders or old policemen, wise. In the air you heard his grating voice and assurance, like a man stepping blithely into traffic looking the wrong way. He liked to drink and was given to extravagant gestures ...

∽

His first words to me that I recall were at a briefing. I was flying as his wingman on my second combat mission. The task of wingman can be easily described: it is to stay with the leader and to look, especially behind—almost all danger comes from there. I knew I was being tried out. I was ready for advice or words of warning. As the aircraft numbers were written next to our names, he commented genially, "Great. You have old No Go, and I've got the Guzzler." They were two of the oldest and slowest airplanes, but he didn't have them changed.

I was fearful as we climbed in the cold air, the planes bobbing slightly. Perhaps it was the day I saw my first MIG, silver, passing above us, complete in every detail, silent as a shark. There were many in the air that day. They were coming from the north in flight after flight, above us. I remember how helpless and alone I felt. My throat was burning as I breathed.

∾

3 March 1952. Fifth mission. Climbed north, going to 40,000 feet. Took up a patrol just below the Yalu. Sky absolutely clear, a deeper blue, like blue ocean. We'd made our first turn when we saw them and dropped tanks. They were coming across the river in flight after flight of from four to six MIGs, above us, at about 45,000. The contrails were heavy and sharp. You could see airplanes fifteen miles away. We turned beneath the MIG trains slowly. Felt acutely that I was in a cockpit deep in enemy territory. Throat dry, burning as I inhaled. Very busy staying with Malone and looking around. Don't recall the sequence but we were in a kind of head-on pass with four of them. They went right over us, close, shiny silver, no red markings, speed fences on the wings, stubby, hostile. We were at 39,000. Two others turned in on us. We turned into them, and as they broke off I called Malone to reverse our turn, but they were too far out.

Don't know how many MIGs there were, perhaps a hundred. We were among them for about fifteen minutes.

∾

Suddenly they were close, and there was no longer any doubt. Cleve felt an awesome disbelief as they passed above him, and he saw the detached-looking tails, like those on the celluloid birds that twirled at circuses.

∾

Soon after leaving the ground, they were crossing patches of stratus that lay in the valleys as heavy and white as glaciers.

Soviet MIG-15 taking off

North for the fifth time. It was still all adventure, as exciting as love, as frightening. Cleve rejoiced in it.

They climbed higher and higher, along the coast. It became difficult to distinguish earth from water where they met. The frozen river mouths blended into white land areas. The rice paddies south of Pyongyang looked like cracked icing on pale French pastry. He saw the knotted string of smoke go back as Desmond test-fired his guns. He checked his own. The sound of them was reassuring.

They climbed into the contrail level. Long, solid wakes of white began flowing behind them. Formations left multiple ribbons of this, streaming sky pennants. Frost formed on the rear of Cleve's canopy. He was chilly, but not uncomfortable. They were north, and he was busy, looking hard, clearing himself, Desmond, and the two other ships in his flight. The sky seemed calm but hostile, like an empty arena. There was little talking.

In half an hour they had reached the Yalu, an unreal boundary winding far below. The sun was higher now. The sky was absolutely clear. His sunglasses made it a deeper blue, like deep ocean. He could see a hundred miles into a China that ended only with a vast horizon, beyond the lives of ten million rooted people. At forty thousand feet they patrolled north and south, turning each time in great, shallow sweeps.

∽

Smooth fields of snow mottled everything, and the rivers were as pronounced as veins, but he did not think of an ancient mother of men. His eye was the flyer's. He saw the hostile mountains, the absence of good landmarks, and the few places flat enough to land in an emergency.

⚮

There is the reservoir, the ice of its wide surface crazed with dark lines. It looks like death invading the tissue—all is disorder, all has failed. You can gaze at it for only a few seconds— the sky seems dead, too, abandoned, but can come alive at any moment with fateful glints.

⚮

Fighters don't fight, as St.-Exupéry said, they murder. He did not fly one himself—he spoke as their possible victim, which in the end he became.

⚮

War is so many things. It is an opportunity to see the upper world, great houses that have become hospitals or barracks, precious objects sold for nothing, families with ancient names at the mercy of quartermaster sergeants. In the familiar footage the guns jump backwards as they fire, the tanks roll past and forgotten men wave. It is all this and also the furnace of the individual in a way that a life of labor is not. Its demands are unending, its pleasures cruel. Goya knew them, and Thucydides, and Isaac Babel. One morning there is the wonderful smell of breakfast, and on the next the sudden arrest and hasty sentencing. The fate that seemed impossible, the justice Lorca knew. He could not cry out. I am a poet! They know he is an intellectual, or worse. They put him in a truck and he rides, with others and without a shred of hope, to an outlying district, where he is handed a shovel and told to dig. It is his grave he is digging, and in silence, the silence he will soon be part of, he begins, who was raised in his country, who became its very voice. *Death laid eggs in the wound,* he once wrote, *at five in the afternoon. His wounds were burning like suns, at five in the afternoon, and the crowd was breaking the windows.* . . . In his grip is the smooth wooden handle, and the first shovelful of earth is one of the most precious moments of his life, if only it could last. But in war nothing lasts and the poets are killed together with the farm boys, the flies feast on their faces.

For us it was simple and always the same: Who was scheduled, what was the weather, what had the earlier missions seen?

∽

10 March 1952. Cool, spring morning. On mobile control. To the south the jagged hills fading in the early mist. A trail of dust behind every vehicle and as ships come over the end of the runway to land, tail-low, the dust puffs up behind them. Thoughts of women. Stretches of idleness, then two deadstick landings come in, both hot, the first one too high and side-slipping on final.

It turns out that one of them had flamed out over Haeju. He and his wingman had been run down to the deck by a lone MIG, a tiger who fired out on the wingman even while the leader was hitting *him!* The wingman, out of fuel, tried to put his ship down on the beach at Cho-do, saw he couldn't make it over some rocks and tried to turn and go the other way but hit and burned.

∽

In the cockpit, Korea

Airplanes had their own personalities. They were not mere mechanical objects but possessed temperaments and traits. Some were good in gunnery, others hopeless. Some were always ready to fly, others rarely. Some planes, if not creaking like ships, nevertheless made strange noises. Without minds or hearts, they were somehow not wholly inanimate. An airplane did not belong to one pilot, like a horse, but to all communally. There were no secrets—pilots talked freely about the behavior of planes and in time flew most of them.

∾

14 March 1952. Honaker was killed today. Crashed about twenty miles to the east. He was testing a troublesome plane, called out something like "I can't stay with it."

Almost got killed myself. Colman and I were coming back from an uneventful mission. Turning final at about 150 knots and 600 feet, the stick froze. Used both hands and couldn't move it. I was in a descending bank towards the ground. I turned off the boost. Nothing. Stick still rigid. I knew I was going to die. I thought of trying the trim. Awful seconds until I realized it wasn't on the stick in this old model but on the side panel. Fumbled for it, still going down, at no more than 300 feet. No effect. I punched off my drop tanks, pulled up the landing gear, flaps, speed brakes. Suddenly the stick gave, began to move. Still in a bank I climbed, curved up into the sky. At 2,000 feet turned on the boost again. Controls were fine. Only with the other hydraulic units in use did the stick freeze.

I declared an emergency and made a long, straight-in, landed with gear down, flaps, and stick absolutely frozen. When I parked my hands were still shaking.

∽

You lived and died alone, especially in fighters. Fighters. Somehow, despite everything, that word had not become sterile. You slipped into the hollow cockpit and strapped and plugged your-

F-86 in flight—Jabara's airplane

self into the machine. The canopy ground shut and sealed you off. Your oxygen, your very breath, you carried with you into the chilled vacuum, in a steel bottle. If you wanted to speak, you used the radio. You were as isolated as a deep-sea diver, only you went up, into nothing, instead of down. You were accompanied. They flew with you in heraldic patterns and fought alongside you, sometimes skillfully, always at least two ships together, but they were really of no help. You were alone. At the end, there was no one you could touch. You could call out to them, as he had heard someone call out one day going down, a pitiful, pleading "Oh, Jesus!" but they could touch you not.

∽

16 March 1952. Mission number 13, an escort. We were at 22,000 covering an RF-80. Bandit trains already reported up. As we crossed the coast near Sinanju there were cons coming south from around Antung.

We turned north and dropped tanks. Suddenly we were in it. Smith turned in on four MIGs. He closed on the last one and began firing.

—You're short! You're short! I called.

Gunsmoke flew back with his exhaust. I was clearing him desperately. The MIG climbed away, smoke or fuel trailing from its right wing.

We turned in behind two other elements. Don't know

where they came from. Sky was full of them. We were closer this time, behind the leader of the trailing element. Smith was firing. There were hits all over the MIG. The wingman was pulling up and away. There was a stream of smoke and we sailed past the MIG; his engine seemed out. Maj. Hnatio later confirmed him crashing. We were past and out of sight.

Smith had fired out. I took the lead. We were low on fuel, less than Bingo (1500 lbs.).

—Just one more time through the area, I said.

—Roger.

But somehow the MIGs had vanished. We were in a gentle left turn and Smith suddenly called,

—Follow me down.

He rolled over, went down, rolled out. There were four MIGs crossing in front of us! Excited, I picked the last one. Was closing too rapidly, reached for the speed brakes, some-how—I don't know how—hit the flap lever unintentionally. Just as I was about to fire, he began pulling away. I fired as he went, discovered my flaps were down. Terrible, stupid feeling. Missed a big chance. Knew there would be others but not like this. I could have had a kill, everything.

∽

He looked over the maps on the walls again, the row of charts, the claims board. The last he stood before for some time. On it was listed the name of every pilot in the group who had ever had a confirmed claim in Korea. Small red stars marked them. There were separate columns for aircraft destroyed, probably destroyed, and damaged, but it was only the first column that really counted. His eye moved down the trail of names. Many of them he did not recognize. They had left the group long before. Some belonged to dead men. There was Robey's, with five stars after it. Nolan had three. Bengert, seven. Imil, six. Tonneson had thirteen, two full lines on the board. And there was his own name with one, and Pell's. Cleve had seen men come in every day to glance at this board and admire their names on it. It was the roll of honor. Hunter had once told him that he would rather have his there than anything else in the world. It was absurd, and yet impressive. Anything that men would willingly die for had to be considered seriously. From this board, perhaps, or one like it, could come names a nation would seize in its appetite for heroes. For a truly singular record there might be lasting fame.

～

18 March 1952. The most terrible moment must be when the great, empty maw of a MIG slips in behind you, staying there while you turn as hard as you can. You hear nothing, cannot think, your head is jammed down into your shoulders by the Gs and you strain to look behind you, pulling for your life.

21 March 1952. Late afternoon mission. Yellow flight, Smith leading.

—Accumulate. All John flights, accumulate.

It's the weather recall word. I have 1,000 lbs. when Smith sees two MIGs going north and we follow them, Smith firing occasionally, almost to Antung. There he breaks off and we head home. Only then does he discover my transmitter is out. We discover something else. There are six MIGs behind us. We're alone. Can't tell if they're closing on us. We climb slowly to 42,000 as we head south. They're still there. Next time I look, they're gone.

We get a steer from Downing.

—Rock your wings if you have over 800 lbs., Smith calls.

Nothing.

—600 lbs., he says.

Nothing.

—400 lbs.

I rock my wings.

—Roger, he says.

I shut down at Haeju. I have 250 lbs. Smith goes on. I watch him drop further and further below me over the rough surface of the now-solid clouds. I glide from 42,000. It's silent, completely quiet. At about 15,000 I try an air start. Fires right up.

Glimpses of the ground through the overcast. I start down

through it and finally break out over Seoul. I hear the tower and other aircraft. They're clearing the area, believing I'm dead-stick.

I can't call. I enter directly onto downwind, land, and taxi in. Less than 100 lbs. when I shut down.

Close enough.

❧

Fuel was measured in gallons in some models of the F-86 and in pounds in other, later ones. The distance from northernmost Korea—the Yalu River—to home was about two hundred miles and minimum safe fuel for the return was about 200 gallons or 1,500 pounds. Planes took off with five or six times this amount, some of it in external tanks that could be jettisoned in favor of speed and maneuverability, but a disproportionate quantity of fuel was used in take-off and climb to altitude.

❧

The bar was crowded. Robey was there, sitting at a table with four or five others and rolling dice for drinks. They were still talking about his last kill, warming him with attention. He received it passively; but there was an aura surrounding him, a cloak of satisfaction. He had been transmuted. He was more than just himself, he was symbolic, as when the sleekness of his ship and the completeness of his equipment so enveloped him that, to a person as near as a wingman or far as a mechanic watching him climb out of sight, he inherited the beauty of his machine.

∽

Speed was everything. If you had speed you could climb or overtake them and, more important, not be easily surprised. You could rid yourself of speed quickly in a number of ways, but to obtain it, especially in the instant it was needed, was impossible.

By subsequent standards these were uncomplicated airplanes, but they could fly above forty-five thousand feet and, going straight down, flirt with the speed of sound. There was a second red needle on the airspeed indicator that moved to mark the limit beyond which you were not supposed to fly though we often did, the needles crossed by thirty or forty knots, usually at low altitude or in a dive, the ship bucking and trying to roll. "On the Mach"—the absolute limit and a favorite phrase.

The difference between our planes and theirs was in most ways insignificant, but in one, crucial. They had cannon—the maw of a MIG seemed swollen and menacing. We had machine guns, which were almost feminine in comparison; the skin of the ship had faint gouges, like the imprint of a spoon, near the nose where the guns poked through. There were six of them. The cannon shells were as big around as a drinking glass and the damage they could do was severe. Machine-gun bullets, on the other hand, were the size of a finger or wine cork. It was the sledgehammer versus the hose. The hose was more flexible and could be adjusted quickly. The slower-firing cannon could not; you could almost say, Oh, God, between the heavy, glowing shots. Once machine guns had their teeth in something, they chewed rapidly.

∽

"Lead, they're shooting at us!"
"That's OK, they're allowed to do that."

∽

The wing commander looked like a fading jockey and had the uncommon name of Thyng. He had piercing blue eyes and wore eagles that because of his smallness seemed doubly large. I can hear his voice as his plane suddenly whips over on its back. "MIGs below us, fellows," he cries. Down we go.

Colman stood before him with a respectfulness untinged by the least subservience. He was, after all, only tossing the dice. He was that dauntless figure, a free man. Soldier, yes, but only occasional soldier; it was all somehow implicit in the crispness of his salute, his effort to be unsmiling, his stained flying suit. He was an experienced fighter pilot and had been an ace in China only seven years earlier. At the moment, he explained, he was in fighter-bombers, which was a waste of his talent; he would like to come to the Fourth.

Thyng was always on the lookout for able men. Did he have any time in F-86? he asked Colman. Yes, sir, Colman said, about two hundred hours. He actually had none and had merely picked a figure that seemed probable. Thyng, interested, told him to leave his name and other details with the adjutant and he would see what could be done.

A few weeks later orders for the transfer came through and Colman left for Korea carrying, he said, at his own suggestion, his flight records with him. These records, sometimes sent separately, are a pilot's full credentials and are sacred. They list everything—every flight, date, weather, type of aircraft. En route to Korea, Colman slid open the window of the transport plane and casually dropped this dossier into the sea. The pages, torn apart, slid under. Fishes nosed at the Japanese planes shot down, night flights in Georgia and Florida, rail-cuts near Sinanju, the entirety.

In the new squadron, the one I was soon afterwards to join, he was asked for his records. They were being mailed, he said blandly. In the meantime, for convenience, he offered a rough breakdown of his time, very close to the fact but including several hundred hours in the F-86. Like the bill in a fine restaurant it was an impressive sum.

Airplanes are the same in the way that ships and automobiles are the same; they are similar, but there are also specifics. On his first flight Colman climbed into the cockpit and after a few minutes beckoned the crew chief to him. It had been a while since he'd flown this model and he didn't want to make a mistake; why didn't the crew chief show him the correct way to start the engine? he asked. The rest was easy—radio, controls, instruments, all these were the usual. He taxied out behind his leader and off they went on a local flight. They were carrying drop tanks but Colman hadn't found out how to turn them on. As they were flying along about forty minutes later, he saw every needle suddenly wilt. His engine had stopped.

He had a flame-out, he reported.

"Roger," the leader said. "Try an air start."

This was another gap in his knowledge. "Just so I do it right," Colman said, "read it to me off the checklist, will you?"

Item by item they went through the procedure. Nothing happened. The engine was all right and there was plenty of fuel, but it was all in the drop tanks. They tried a second time and then declared an emergency. Colman would have to try and make a dead-stick landing.

He might have done it easily except he was a little short of altitude. Nothing can amend that. At the last, seeing he was not going to make it, he picked out the best alternative he could, railroad tracks, and landed on them wheels-up, which was the right way. He was skating down the rails as if they were a wet street, finally coming to a stop just inside a wire-mesh gate which happened to be the entrance to the salvage yard. The plane, damaged beyond repair, would have ended up there anyway. Eventually the fire trucks came, and an ambulance, and Colman, who had injured his back slightly, was taken to the hospital.

One of the first things noticed in the wreckage was that the drop-tank switches had not been turned on. Amell was in a very unfriendly mood when he arrived at the hospital. As soon as he entered the room, Colman held up his hands defensively. "Major, you don't have to say it," he began, "I fucked up. I know I fucked up. But you have to admit one thing. *After* I fucked up, nobody could have done a better job."

Impudence saved him. He was in disgrace but at the same time admired. You could not help liking his nerve.

❧

We traveled far together, sometimes to forbidden places, deeper and deeper into Manchuria, almost to Mukden, looking for them in the sanctuary, so high that the earth seemed neuter. It was a great, barren country, brown, without features. The Yalu was behind us, no longer in sight. Farther and farther north. Every minute was ten miles. No one would know

Capt. Philip "Casey" Colman

what had happened to us, no one would ever hear. My eye returned to the fuel gauge again and again. The needle never moved but then it would be lower. How much do you have? he asks. Nine hundred pounds, I reply. Two brief clicks of the mike; he understood. Finally, giving up, we turned.

☙

It was not duty, it was desire. Duty would not search with such avidity in the waning light, coming down the river one last time, the earth already in darkness that was rising slowly, like a tide, the heavens being the last to go. A strange high sound begins in the earphones: gun-laying radar. Along the river a final time. Near its mouth the darkened earth begins to light up, first in one place and then another, like a city come to life. Soon the entire ground is flashing. They are firing at us far below. Black shellbursts, silent, appear around us, some showing an unexpected red core.

It was victory we longed for and imagined. You could not steal or be given it. No man on earth was rich enough to buy it and it was worth nothing. In the end it was worth nothing at all.

༄

24 March 1952. The dawn mission got into a big fight. I was walking to the showers when I heard that Schwab had been hit by a 23mm.

The second mission got into an even bigger fight. We heard it at lunch. Woody was hit in the wing. Carey was shot down. First we heard he was missing. After a while his fuel would have been gone.

Col. Mahurin gave us a ride down to the line. He was eager to go on the next mission. So were we.

None of us saw anything. We were at fever pitch and saw absolutely nothing. Tremendous letdown.

༄

When the ships returned from a mission, everybody watched for them. Usually, they came lining back to the field in flights of four, flying tight show formation with the black smoke fading in parallel streams behind as they turned in towards the runway and landing pattern. They seemed to be most indestructible then. They were of frozen silver. Nothing could possibly dim that grace. No enemy could deny them. Departures were stirring; but every return, even the most uneventful, was somehow transcendent and a call to the heart to rise in joy. Out of the north they had come again, brief strokes of splendor.

∽

6 April 1952. 25th mission. Kasler on my wing. Five days ago, when I was over at Tsuiki, ferrying, he shot down a MIG and damaged another.

Love is leading the flight. I'm determined to get a kill. Casey and Austin each had one on the mission before this.

We climb north through layers of stratus out over the Yellow Sea. MIG flights being reported in the area.

Blue Flight is in a fight near Mizu. We turn east past Antung at 30,000. Moments later there are planes below us going west. We drop tanks and go down. They're 86s.

Meanwhile, Love had gone on and run into MIGs. I could have kicked myself. We see six or eight 86s, nothing more. Kasler talking a lot, making suggestions. Someone calls ten

MIGs over Sinanju at 23,000. We head there. I spot two flecks of silver, low, going north.

—Stay with me, I call, peeling down.

They're straight-winged, ours. Climb back up, low on fuel, heading north again. The sun is low, the earth becoming shadowed. We hear that MIGs are attacking our fighter-bombers near Long Dong. Head there, find nothing. Two ships near the river trailing thin lines of black smoke. 86s, chasing a MIG.

Suddenly a plane flashes by just beneath us, very close, a MIG! I rack it over to get behind and cut him off. Calmer than ever before. Cage my gunsight and look back to clear Kasler who cries,

—Check your right! Look right!

There's another MIG, the wingman, not two hundred feet away, stubby, foreign-looking, like a great, silent fish. I turn towards him and start to "S" back.

—Break left! I hear Kasler call. They're coming in on you from the left!

I break, don't see them, roll out to pick up the MIG again. He was about 1,800 feet away now. I fire but see no hits. Finally have to break off. We're about forty miles inside China. I have 1,000 pounds. Time it takes to cross back over the river seems interminable.

∞

The engines drank as they climbed. It was a hemorrhage. They were paying for altitude with an open-throated flow. It poured away. The needle of the gauge seemed to fail as Cleve looked at it. The minutes were endless. He suffered through them, trying not to think, restraining himself. He looked out to sea, where they would probably end up. It had always seemed a sanctuary. Now it was unnerving, a place to drown in. He thought of bailing out. He had never left an airplane before, and the moment of abandoning that close cockpit for sheer, climactic space chilled him.

They were climbing fast. The ships performed better the emptier they became, and the blackfaced dial then showed just less than one hundred pounds. It was hardly enough to wet the bottom of the tank.

∽

8 April 1952. To Tokyo for R and R, Woody, Austin, Kasler, and I. Tried to catch an earlier flight at K-16 but nothing available. Ate at the mess in our blues, then went to the club. Maj. Amell there, having a few. Sat down with him. Soon he was wishing he could go with us, he had a head cold and couldn't fly anyway. He called for a staff car for us, insisted that we stay in Japan until the 15th. We said, largely in self-defense, we would, but only if he came with us. By god, he would!

He called Col. Thyng and in fifteen minutes was back in

blues with a B4 bag. When the staff car came, Casey saw us off, firing shots in the air. It emptied the movie, but we were gone.

Miserable flight. Canvas seats, cold cabin, impossible to sleep. Took off at one in the morning and sat shivering in the darkness until five AM.

Astor Hotel, bar and restaurant open 24 hours, Japanese not allowed. Slept until afternoon, then downtown to the Meiji Building. No one I knew was in FEAF anymore, only Betsy Vandegrift in Flying Safety. Then to the Gae-jo-en. Drinking. Amell talked and talked. Woody nicknamed him Rackety-Rax, should be back in college as an undergraduate.

On to the Imperial. Singing songs in the bar, Amell shouting "Louder!" People began to leave. The manager came. Amell was telling some civilians he didn't want to impress them with his education. Then to the Mimatsu, big nightclub on the Ginza. Huge floorshow, hostesses in evening gowns, confetti from exploding firecrackers, Amell smashing martini glasses on the floor.

Miyoshi's again. A girl smooth as a pear. In the morning I hesitated outside, thinking I'd forgotten something. Woody asked if I was going back to get my self-respect. Found out that Amell had spent the night sleeping in the backseat of a car at Tachikawa. Met him at the Marinouchi Hotel. He didn't want to have lunch. Said his friends in the past never had enough money to eat and drink, too. Drinks, shrimp cocktails, and steaks. Bill was $1.80. Amell off to Tachikawa to visit the nurses again. We went to the Bacchus, an officers' nightclub. The strippers took everything off, the last one at the beginning of her act. Great-looking girls. Heard they were asking 20,000 yen for the night. At the Hotel Sakiya tried to buy a wonderful wind-up gramophone. Bought five bicycles the next day instead, went back to the Bacchus.

Shopped the last day, went out to Tachikawa, Kasler, Woody, and I. Had a steak dinner and flew out at midnight. Miserable flight. No sleep. Landed at Seoul at 5:30 in the morning. It was Easter Sunday. Flew a mission that afternoon, my 26th. Saw nothing.

15 April 1952. The rains have come and high winds. Windows rattle incessantly. Once in a while the door blows open. No flying. We work to fix up the room.

∽

There were so many things that could happen, a large part was chance. Perhaps it has rained for days—the planes sit out in the weather and dampness affects them, the radios become unreliable. *Break*! they are crying in a fight and you hear nothing. The silence is uncanny. *Break right*! they are shouting, *break right*! For some reason you look back and there, behind you, is an intake the size of a locomotive. In fright you pull too hard and the plane shudders, snaps, begins to spin. The earth is revolving, dirt from the cockpit floor is floating up, and they are following you down; when you pull out at low speed they'll be waiting.

There were days one felt a dread, when something was wrong, something impalpable. Like a beast lying in a field sensing danger, you could not run from it, you did not even know what it was. It was an eclipse, not total, of courage. People were getting hit, Woody, Bambrick, Straub. Carey was lost, Honecker. Sharp, with his savoir-faire and black moustache, was shot down—the MIG dropping out of the clouds behind him—and rescued.

∞

17 April 1952. Sunny. Promising. On the early mission, weather reccy, Bryant and Miller were hit by MIGs. They reported the enemy fields jammed with aircraft.

At the briefing, Col. Thyng said there were 600 of them counted on Antung, Ta-tung-kou, and Taka-shan. Flew three missions, leading the flight on the third. Our squadron took off first. We went to 42,000 over the river, throttled back and slowly descended, east to west, then back again, .85 or .9 all the way. They were reporting MIGs in the air. Lattshaw saw

Col. Harrison R. Thyng, CO 4th Fighter Wing, Korea, 1952

streams of fuel and vapor from their dropped tanks near Mizu. We were halfway there at 36,000. The MIGs were said to be at 25,000. We passed Mizu but saw nothing, turned back towards the southeast. After a minute or two, there they were, skipping north through the cons. One was at 12 o'clock. I turned in behind him.

—That's a MIG, Jim, Austin said.

It was turning and climbing, white cirrus behind it. Big barn of a tail. I fired, but my gunsight was terrible. With the pipper right on him, my tracers were arcing out far to the left, even in fixed sight. I couldn't pull closer. May have hit him but doubt it. Finally I was just following.

—We may have to break, Kasler called.

A few seconds later,

—Break left, Orange!

Two MIGs coming down on us, turning in behind.

—They're breaking off, I called. Kas, reverse your turn.

They climbed away. We circled slowly, hunting. Near the river we spotted two, but with 86s behind them, Austin and Flanagan.

—Get after that one at two o'clock, Austin called. I hit him, but I'm fired out.

I turned that way. The MIG was too far off. Kasler had called MIGs at twelve o'clock, low, but I didn't hear. We became split up. We headed for the mouth of the river to join again, needles crossed by 30 knots. Swung north again after joining, but we were low on fuel. I had only 200 gallons. We saw nothing.

Will I never get one?

20 April 1952. First morning mission. Weather not good. Near Pyongyang shreds of cirrus hung in the air like icicles on the edge of a roof. Ahead, the mist was flat as a table. A band of green haze rimmed the distant horizon.

Near Antung, a great, many-layered cloud, like an immense fungus. We were up for an hour and three quarters but saw nothing.

21 April 1952. Big fight this morning. Casey and I sighted two.

—Take the one on the left, he said.

But they turned left, and he took the left one. The other curved away and down.

I cleared him and watched the two of them against dark blue sky, climbing, turning, diving in majestic loneliness and silence. Casey was firing but not hitting him. I was crossing to the inside of the turn, slightly ahead. I called that it was me crossing in front.

—OK, go ahead, you take him, Casey said.

I was sure Casey would get him and didn't want to share his kill.

—No, go on, I said.

A few moments later Casey asked if I had the MIG in sight. No.

—I've lost him, he said.

We flew along the river. Saw one plane splash in a bright burst of flame and black smoke. Turned out to have been Kasler's MIG. We dove on a MIG, lost it, then on another. We were north of the river, near Antung, going almost straight down at .95, even Mach 1, leveling out below 1,000 feet as the MIG landed. We went across Antung on the deck. My heart was pounding. Crossed back over the Yalu near the mouth and headed back. I could hear them talking. Love had gotten two, Straub one, Kasler one.

DeArmont had been shot down. He was on Amell's wing. They broke, but the MIGs turned inside them. The cannons hit him. His wing was on fire. He bailed out, they saw his chute open.

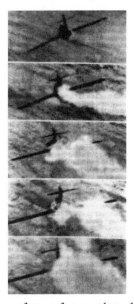

Gun camera footage of MIG-15 being destroyed

Talked with Casey about the MIG at Antung. "His wheels are down!" I'd called. Casey grinned with yellowing teeth—the cigars.

—If he'd bounced once, I'd have gotten him.

In the afternoon I led an element. Cirrus haze at 30,000 feet. Smooth, milk sea and above it cloudless sky. We conned across it—eternity. MIGs were up, but we couldn't find them. Came home in the dusk, low on fuel, Austin and I, unsuccessful.

28 April 1952. Sometimes at night, uneasiness. The states are far away, many missions. Thinking of Miyoshi's, the spare, clean rooms, the deference. Once more before the end, I think.

∽

The mind could occupy itself, but the dumb, quavering heart could do nothing. Cleve sat in the cockpit, checking the second hand on his wristwatch. He drummed his fingers on the tight metal skin of the ship. Finally, it was time to start engines. He passed gratefully into the realm of function.

Once they were into it, the sky was clear, and bright sunny blue. It was a sky, Cleve thought, you could see tomorrow in. He looked over towards Hunter on his wing. DeLeo was flying number three, wide on the opposite side, just then moving into position with Pell number four out beyond him. They climbed north, over the quiet Haeju Peninsula and then across the edge of the Yellow Sea, heading the shortest way for Antung.

A fight seemed to have started already. They could hear the loud, excited transmissions of one flight among the MIGs. They were late, Cleve thought angrily. He pushed the nose of his ship down slightly, lowering the rate of climb and increasing the forward speed. He wanted to get to the Yalu as soon as possible.

∽

He felt a buoyancy that was both fear and expectation. From here on, he was working against time to find them. He headed up the river, passing occasional elements, all friendly. He scanned the wide sky meticulously, high and low. There was a speck of dirt on the plexiglass canopy that looked like a distant airplane every time his eye passed over it. Despite himself, it tricked him again and again. Aside from that, there was nothing. As he turned to go down towards the mouth of the river he saw four ships chasing two MIGs far below, flashes of silver against the snowy ground. The radio was cluttered increasingly with cries of battle.

"Bandit train number six leaving Antung."

It seemed impossible to be traveling through so big a fight

Leaving squadron locker room for a mission

without finding anything. A desperate sensation of futility seized him. He was certain he was heading in the wrong direction, but he had turned less than a minute before. He could not cover ground fast enough. He felt as if he were merely hanging in air.

❧

30 April 1952. Terrible day. We were on alert and scrambled to cover a downed F-80 pilot near Sinanju. On the way north a fake Dentist Charlie was reporting MIGs, "Ko-shun Flight, Jackpot Flight"—between Pyongyang and Anju. They were supposed to be at 30,000. We squirmed in our seats, banked, saw nothing.

We were cruising, not very fast, at about 85%, near Sinanju, working slowly north. Suddenly there were two MIGs coming down behind us, close together, that dull smooth gray.

—Break left, Casey! I called.

He hesitated for a moment to look back and in that second was hit twice, once by an explosive shell.

I heard Austin,

—Where do you have them, Jim?

A moment later, he called to his leader,

—Break left, Kas! Break left! *For Christ's sake, break left!*

The last was so convincing that Casey and I momentarily broke left again.

The MIGs hadn't followed us. We'd reversed, but they had too much speed. We followed them for 40 or 50 miles but never gained. I fired a few times but with no apparent results. Near the river we saw six more to the west. Then two more were turning in behind us. We were at about 35,000. We started turning with them. Passed canopy to canopy halfway around. After another 180 they dove and we started getting behind them. Casey was leading again by then. We were at .95 or more. The MIGs began to pull up, then split. One turned

towards Antung, the other dove towards the Sui-Ho reservoir.
We followed the second but Casey's oxygen hose became
unbuckled. He caught it when his vision became blurred, but
we lost the MIG.

We leveled out. Two more MIGs were coming in behind
us. I called them out, two or three thousand feet back. Casey
began a slight turn to the left. The MIGs were gaining. He
turned right momentarily. They were 1,500 feet back.

—Break one way or the other, Casey! I called.

He broke left. Too late. They were following close, firing.
Their noses lit up as they sailed around behind us like toys on
a string. Their tracers were arcing between Casey and me. We
were literally flying between the rounds, I don't know how. My
heart was pounding, and at the same time it was as if I were
watching it all from above. Behind us they had the scent of the
kill, they could see the strikes; nothing would dislodge them. I
was in panic but also calm, as if observing from some higher,
safer place. We were turning as hard as we could and they were
turning with us. The altimeter was unwinding. Straining to
look back, I could see them, steady and unmoving, like the
pods behind you on an amusement park ride that rise when
you rise and go down when you go down, mechanical and
effortless.

Somehow we had pulled ahead a little. We were flying too
desperately for them to lead us. The other element was call-

ing—they could hear us—to ask where we were and whether they could help us, but neither Colman nor I could answer. It was pitiless. It was like being held by a python—the least relinquished space, it constricts to hold. We were being crushed in boundless air.

The break had been into me, and I lost Casey, he didn't keep me in sight though he should have. I was diving, pulling 6 or 7 Gs, straining to look back. Finally I saw the two MIGs split and climb away. I was down to 10,000 feet. I held it on the Mach and climbed towards the sea.

At 25,000 picked up Casey near Chong-ju. We headed home together. I had 40 gallons at 30,000 feet, about 35 miles from the field. I went in first, made a quick pattern, turned onto final at 170. I was too high. I slipped to lose altitude but hit hot and long. Maybe it was nerves, delayed reaction. I was on the brakes immediately but couldn't stop. Somehow I didn't consider going around, I was so certain of stopping. In mobile, they thought my engine was running high; they thought I had added power and was going around. A lurch as a tire blew. The end of the runway was coming up. I suddenly thought I'll just turn at the end, onto the taxiway, but as I did, almost relieved, the right landing gear folded under the strain. The wing hit and buckled.

The fire trucks and Col. Thyng and Casey drove up.

—Nice work, the colonel said coldly. You know how badly

we need airplanes, too. You were hot as hell. What a pattern. I saw the whole thing.

He had me put my gear in the car. We drove off.

—Colonel, I could cry, I said, absolutely shamed.

—Well, he said more calmly, at least it's an old A.

They wrote it off as a combat loss, the low fuel, a damaged plane just behind me, plus the high idle of the engine. I wasn't charged with an accident. I told Col. Mahurin I would make it up to him.

᠖

"D" Flight 335th Squadron, left to right, Salter, James Low, Albert Smiley, Coy Austin, Philip Colman

4 May 1952. The worst feeling of all is when flights come back with no tanks and noses blackened from firing—they have gotten MIGs. Late today Colman and Kasler each got their third, Mattson his fourth.

9 May 1952. Winter is over. Mornings are quiet and dreamy. Guys moving cots outdoors to take sunbaths. Woody pointed out three small locust trees turning green between the barracks.

∽

On takeoff, he noticed for the first time that the rice paddies surrounding Kimpo were turning green. He watched the ground flowing beneath him. There was one small farm that had three tall poplars in front of the house giving it shade. They swept across it. Now, in motion, he felt somewhat better. They picked up speed and began to climb. He was aware of an elusive, mystic sensation supporting the physical as they went up.

It was a beautiful day. The coarse, brown peninsula looked peaceful. The snow had vanished from the mountains, and the rivers were free of ice. The sea was like an immense piece of jade through his sunglasses. Along the many crestlines were veins that gleamed like silver when the sun hit them. Thick green crowns were beginning to appear, and even the clay and sand seemed brighter. Low, scattered puffs of clouds looked like foam flecks on an even surf.

∽

Free of the gravitational forces of reality, he sat in the sunshine and looked out over a crystal empire. Antung lay under a dome of clear air that reached every horizon. The river, its bridges, and the earthen town beside it were as small as a history book map. It was almost sleep-inducing. He knew a tranquility as timeless as a dream of deepest waters. If death were ever to touch him here, it would be with a gesture of equality, with fingertips only. In this high, sterile realm he would fight and, conquering, it seemed, become immortal.

∽

15 May 1952. Sultry morning. As we withdraw from the Yalu they are calling MIGs taking off—five bandit flights heading south, but it's too late for us, we're low on fuel, just enough to get back.

Walking across the ramp after debriefing, I hear the news—the alert flight has gotten three MIGs. That's Casey, Low, Kasler, and Smiley. Near Ops, Van Herschberger confronts me. Have I heard the news? Kasler shot down two! He's made ace!

Sudden, fierce heartbreak. Juvenile, perhaps, but unquenchable. Smiley had gotten the third MIG.

They were still in the air. I didn't want to be at the debriefing and have to congratulate them, I didn't have the courage.

As I passed the firing-in butt, two planes were completing their landing roll and turning off the runway. I recognized Casey's dark, leather helmet in the first one. His gun ports were clean. Low's also. Another two ships were just rolling to the end of the strip. Both with blackened gun ports. Kasler and Smiley. It was true.

With James Kasler, later to win three AF crosses

Later I went down to D Flight to congratulate them. Kasler was radiant. Col Thyng had jumped up on his wing to congratulate him.

~

The single daring act—it was hard to imagine the enormous distance that it placed between us. The fifth was more than just another; it was beatification, the step across the gulf. On the tail of another plane at top speed, determined, closer than one dared, not knowing the other pilot or what he would do, down to the treetops, to the fatal earth—I had flown this very flight myself, it had been my initiation though I hardly imagined repeating it in war. Kasler had his fifth, but more than that, he had reorded the state of things; he had begun like me, as a gunbearer, and now was where boldness had placed him, on the other side.

~

About 17 May 1952. Col. Mahurin shot down today. He seemed absolutely indestructible, twenty or more victories in Europe, smiling, enthusiastic, a group commander at thirty-two. It was at Sinanju and he was on fire, whether from flak or MIGs nobody knows for sure. He may have bailed out, but the wingman never saw it.

swelled. There was nothing to compare with the happiness of leading. Towards the final test and winnowing they flew together, and though a man on the ground could neither see nor hear them, they were up, specks of metal moving through a prehistoric sky, contaminating an ocean of air with only their presence, electrifying the heavens. Cleve felt a distilled fulfillment. For these moments, no price could be too high.

As they neared the Yalu, the cloudiness increased, and above a spotty floor of white there was one huge cumulus buildup, a towering mushroom of brightness as big as a county. It looked like a cosmic fungus, like layers of wrath. They were at forty thousand feet then and climbing. The river was still five minutes away. Suddenly, cutting through the lesser voices, there was Colonel Imil's.

"Dust on the runway at Antung, boys," he called. "Heads up."

It was as if they had waited for him, Cleve thought slowly. He tried to see the reddish plumes rising, but the cumulus was in the way. Beyond that vast cloud and beneath it, they were taking off to fight. He began searching the sky with the intensity of a man who has lost a diamond on a public beach.

෨

24 June 1952. Left the briefing nervous. Dressed, flight briefing. Finally we were off. North in ominous silence. Far below glimpses of the straight-winged fighter-bombers. Explosions were hiding the dam in smoke. Not a MIG in the air. It was as if they didn't exist. The fires burned into the next day. Not a ship lost to either ground fire or enemy aircraft. We landed in disappointment.

4 July 1952. Fighter-bombers going north again today. Target the North Korean Officers' Academy about 25 miles south of the Mizu. First good weather in a week. My 89th mission.

We're at 25,000, watching the fighter-bombers move evenly across the green earth and hills. Enemy trains being called out. Air is flashing with F-86s.

Suddenly, MIGs called out along the river. Then Low calls them at 30,000, heading along the Yalu. We drop tanks and begin climbing through a layer of scattered cirrus. All at once the MIGs are on us, coming in from 8 o'clock, slightly high. Cope is on my right. We break into them. They pass behind us and are immediately lost from sight as we continue to turn and roll out at 22,000.

MIGs being called out everywhere, the radio is cluttered with cries. Someone says there are many south of the Mizu at 24,000. We head that way, 86s all around. Search for three or four minutes.

We're turning north again when we see two to the west,

heading south. We turn, fall in behind them a mile or so back. We'll never catch them, but then they chandelle up to the right and we gain on them by Immelmaning up between them and the river. I'm behind and slightly beneath the leader, about 1,500 feet back. He turns to the right. I duck my head, can't find the gunsight reticle—we're pulling Gs and it's off the glass. As we level, it swims into view. I fire a burst. The tracers fall short.

He begins to climb and turn and I cut him off, firing and closing. At about 1,100 feet, some hits in the right wing and a few moments later, at less than 1,000, I get a solid burst into his fuselage. Intense, bright flases.

He rolls over. I push forward, still shooting, hitting him. Suddenly the canopy flies off. A second later the pilot, a compact bundle, comes out.

I shout to Cope.

—Did you see that?

—Roger.

We watch the MIG spin down from 30,000 feet, very leisurely, until finally in some wooded hills its shadow rises to meet it and it hits and explodes.

We're below Bingo, with 200 gallons. We head back.

My first MIG, after these months of heartache and trying.

On this mission, the Fourth claimed six MIGs. Two of our planes were lost, Jolley and Beetle who was on his second mis-

Captain Troy Cope

sion. They got into trouble up north, Jolley was hit and heading for the water when Beetle was hit, too. They were very low on fuel. I heard one of them say, "500 pounds." They bailed out over the water near Cho-do. Jolley was picked up but Beetle drowned.

If it hadn't been for one man, Low, who had spotted the MIGs taking off and called them out, things might have been very different, Col. Thyng said.

∞

10 July 1952. Woody said good-bye this morning. Watched him go with genuine sorrow. In the afternoon, my 92nd mission.

Tremendous heat. Sat in the cockpit bathed in sweat, the oxygen mask slippery with it.

The north seemed serene and unthreatening. MIGs called out between Antung and Anju. Flew along the river near a huge cumulus build-up that covered the entire area and beneath a lean shelter of clouds that formed a tunnel 20,000 feet high along the Yalu. Hoped to catch them coming back or others heading south but saw nothing.

Came home, climbing fast, clean through the empty air, over the water, just Drukenbrodt and I. Felt again how heartbreaking to leave.

11 July 1952. MIGs were being called up, but nobody saw them until we were nearly to the river. Then the excitement. Somebody chasing a pair north, didn't think they could catch them. Somebody else, Dog, screamed to break. We dropped tanks. Spotted a single, to the north and west, across the setting sun. Headed for him. It was a good area to be in when the MIGs came home. I was sure we would intercept them.

I lost the single. We turned towards the river. Flew around a thunderstorm there and looked in. Through the gray rain ships were climbing and diving like gnats under a streetlight. Went on, spotted two more, turned after them and lost them in the cloud.

20 July 1952. Big fight this time. Col. Baker was Red Flight, first off. He was to cover the airfields. I was John Yellow, far back. On the way north I could hear him going after some. Finally he said something like "Dust in center field, boys," then nothing more.

Blue Flight dropped tanks for a flight of six above them at 36,000. Soon we ran into MIGs ourselves. Chased two for a

2nd Lt. James F. Low, in the course of the extraordinary record he made in Korea

while, gave up, turned west along the river, then back east again. Two MIGs crossed above us, heading north. Turned after them. Fell in about 2,000 feet back and the same below. Jones had a slow ship. The MIGs turned. I cut them off and gained, but Jones was falling behind. He was barely in sight. Then he called, there were twelve MIGs behind him, he said.

Did we have a better chance at them, I asked? He didn't know. We continued on. Finally Jones lost me. I was alone. Heard the weather recall being given. I was closer than ever to the MIGs. They began another turn, to the right. I asked Jones if he had me. He thought he did. He was at 9 o'clock, he said. I looked but couldn't see him. I heard him cry,

—Hey, that's a MIG!

He'd joined up with one by mistake. He swung in to try and get a shot but it climbed away.

I was very close now, just one more turn from being in range. I cleared myself as well as I could. I felt very alone. Watched as two more MIGs came down from 3 o'clock high and joined the two I was chasing. Then they climbed back out to the right. Was sure they were going to come in on me but they must have lost sight of me. Didn't see them again.

I was very far north and down to minimum fuel. I had to break it off. Began a gradual turn towards home at 40,000. As I did, I was horrified to see the MIGs turn, too. They had never done that before.

I was at 100% and going .95 in an A (#158). Antung was at least seventy miles ahead. I was weaving slightly, looking behind me. Saw two other MIGs turning far below, on the deck. Couldn't do anything about it. A minute later, another one down there. I hadn't seen them low for months. Then, suddenly, I saw tanks falling to both left and right, from above. Searched for the MIGs dropping them, but couldn't find them. Another pair of tanks fell, pale, curling trails, at 2 o'clock, and behind them came a MIG. Probably misjudged his pass because of my speed and slight dive. He swung in a good way back and began firing. The rounds were dropping short, below me. At last I crossed over Sinuiju at 10,000 feet and began climbing slowly out towards the sea.

Druckenbrodt had become separated, too. He was at 20,000 over Pyongyang with 100 gallons. I told him to climb to 30,000. He was getting steers from Dentist, 180, then 200, then 220 degrees.

At 30,000 he reported 60 gallons. I told him to shut it down at 50 and save that for making the field. A rain squall was moving in rapidly from the south. K-13 was already closed in.

I landed and sat in the cockpit near the squadron area listening to the radio. The storm was almost at the far end of the runway, huge, gray mass. I alerted GCA to try and pick him up. The ceiling was coming down fast. Finally he appeared to the north, coming in on initial. Had a terrible 30 seconds waiting for him to make base leg without flaming out, but he did. It was OK.

Once again, no luck. Four missions left.

❧

He could not tell what it was at first. Far out, a strange, dreamy rain was falling, silver and wavering. It was a group of drop tanks, tumbling down from above, the fuel and vapor streaming from them. Cleve counted them at a glance. There were a dozen or more, going down like thin cries fading in silence.

❧

He was not completely conscious of what he was doing or even planning. A hand that had done this for years was guiding his ship. He was merely riding along, it seemed, striving to see better, to see everything; and he was cutting the MIGs off slightly in the turn, getting inside them. He could distinguish the black markings on the leader. He pulled after him, distended. As he did, still far from being in a position to shoot, he was stricken with a sense of resignation and fear. They went around and around in this silent, unyielding circle. His fuel was getting lower and lower. He glanced quickly at it: seven hundred pounds. They were going down steadily; they had passed through twenty thousand. The airspeed was building. He had lost sight of the other two MIGs, of Hunter, of everything but the winding earth and the lead ship turning with him, motionless as the world spun about them.

❧

The airplanes no longer seemed involved. It was a battle of wills, of the strength to hang on, as if by the teeth alone. To let up meant to lose, and it was Cleve's advantage. He was rigid with the determination to stay there.

Suddenly the MIG rolled over and started down. For an endless part of a second Cleve hesitated, surprised. They were very low. He was not sure he could follow him through and clear the ground. He was almost certain the MIG could not make it. He knew a moment of awful decision, and then rolled and followed. They were going straight down, in a split S, wide open. They burst through the level of clouds. The earth was shooting up at him. The stick seemed rigid. He trimmed and pulled back as hard as he could, popping the speed brakes to help pitch him through. Everything faded into gray and then black. When it began to be gray again, he saw that they had made it. He was right behind Casey, on the deck. The hills and trees were whipping past just beneath them. His ship slammed and jolted crazily against ripples of air.

∽

Late July 1952. Days of rain falling hard, then soft, like layers of gravel. Water everywhere except in the latrine—the pumping station is flooded. K-16 is flooded, too, all the transports and helicopters have come in here temporarily. The hours seem endless. Sitting in the same room, day after day, with nothing to do. Everything leather has green mould.

1 August 1952. First good day in a week. A max effort escort
and sweep. Climbing north through thin layers. Bandit
trains being called out, near Anju, northeast of Anju, north
of Antung, seven in all. Coming up to meet us this first fair
day.

We're at 40,000. Kozey calls MIGs taking off at Antung.
We're too high and far away to go after them. Then Col. Baker
calls MIGs above him.

—Where?

—At the Mizu. Come and get them, Yellow, he says.

—Roger, colonel, we're on the way. What altitude?

—33,000.

We head northeast. To the right is another flight of 86s,
heading the same way, and below specks are wheeling up and
down with each other in a canted Lufberry. When I take my
eyes off them, I lose them. A moment later I see what looks
like many aircraft heading generally west. We turn slightly
north. Then they are streaming beneath us like salmon, MIGs,
many of them, about 5,000 feet below, the perfect bounce.

—MIGs below, I call. Let's go!

We pull around and start down. I have Miller on my wing.
I warn him to keep a good eye out, there are many, many of
them around.

We're closing on a flight of four. They break slightly to the
right and up. I'm cutting off the leader, decide to take the
wingman, who's lagging a little, instead. I roll out briefly, then

in behind the wingman at about 1,500 feet. I hunch over, looking for him in the reticle. An 86, firing, goes by beneath
behind another MIG. A moment later still another, greenish
gray with a Chinese communist or North Korean insignia
pops up almost beside but in front of me to the right. He starts
a slow turn to the left, crossing below my nose, not 500 feet
out. Can't believe my luck. I reverse my turn to get right
behind him as he descends towards the west.

I clear myself quickly to the right. Nothing. Where's
Miller? Now left. There's a MIG just behind, firing, showing a
little of his belly so I can tell he's leading me! He's at 7 o'clock,
enormous, not 300 feet back! I can see his nose flashing and
the lashes of cannon fire whipping by!

—Break left! I cry and pull it in.

There's a second MIG, his wingman, inside of him and
firing, too. We're breaking down from about 35,000, not able
to pull it too tightly. I can see them following me around.
Can't see Miller. I pull harder, it snaps and heads straight
down. I let it go and pull into a turn again a few seconds later
with more airspeed. I look back. Nothing. They're gone.

I call Miller. No answer. Only the radio clamor of a fight,
then an anguished moan. Someone says,

—Oh, Jesus.

It's Miller. I call him again and again. Towards the Mizu an
airplane with a heavy trail of white smoke is going straight

down, near where we'd been fired upon. Miller, I know. Then he answers.

—Roger, he says. I got the MIG that was after you.

We head to the outermost island at Long Dong and finally spot one another at 24,000 feet. He has 230 gallons, I have 250. We head back to the Mizu, climbing, and get to 40,000 but there's nothing left of the fight when we get there. It's vanished completely. It's like visiting a Civil War battlefield.

Back on the ground it turns out that Miller had screamed, "Break left, Yellow Lead!" at me three times, but I had a bad receiver and failed to hear it. Cope heard it, though. The MIGs had just popped up between Miller and me as I was reversing to go after the olive green one and had started firing. Miller thought I was hit. He fired at the MIG, not hitting him until a last burst when the MIG was rolling over to follow me down. The pilot bailed out.

Felix Asla was lost. His wing was shot off south of Mizu, and he was seen spinning rapidly at a long, low angle to the ground. He had four kills, a Silver Star, a couple of DFCs and a spot majority. He'd commanded a squadron for six months and was a favorite of Thyng's, a real tiger. It was his 95th mission. In addition to Asla, five planes were damaged today. Bambrick came back with five hits in his, one of them a 37mm—two in the left wing (one through the gas tank), one in the canopy, one in the tail, and one through the left speed brake.

One more mission to go.

6 August 1952. So strong now, again, the sad feeling of not being part of it, detached, with no stake in things.

Near evening I stand along the ridge that runs behind the barracks and the officers' club, looking towards the runway where they are taking off for the last mission.

Later, they come whistling in, in flights or pairs, peeling off and landing with the sun already down behind the hills.

Today, a Meteor failed to make it off and crashed at the downhill end of 32, going into the Korean huts there and exploding. The pilot was killed. On such a nice, sunny day.

∽

It was like leaving an old love. There was so much more than he could ever remember. He stared down at the hand-sized earth that had drifted by beneath him so slowly every time before. Now he seemed to be crossing it with great speed, as if running with the current of time. Ribbons of ocher road, highlands and villages were all floating swiftly out of sight under the wing. He felt an overwhelming, captive sadness. It was his farewell. He twisted around in the seat to look behind, to see in the unclear corner of his vision just once more the river, the silent, muddy Yalu. It was already far behind and dropping back more every minute, a languid trace of reflection among the hills and flatlands. He had never heard of it before he had come, and the closest he had been to it was a distance to be measured in vertical miles, but he felt that he knew it as well as a familiar street— its mud flats and wide mouth, its bridges, cities, bare banks, islands, and the lonely way it came from the interior. It seemed unbelievable that he would never see it again.

∽

In the end there is a kind of illness. A feeling of inconsequence, even lightness, takes hold. It is, in a way, like the earliest days, the sense of being an outsider. Others are taking one's place, nameless others who can never know how it was. It is being given to them, the war with all its fading, romantic detail, its disasters and lucky chances. They will be coming home through the intense skies of autumn, settling gracefully in over the boundary of the field. The smooth black runway floats up to meet them. The ships are empty, featherlight, the fuel tanks almost drained, the belts of ammunition vanished; they are bringing back nothing except that thing we prized above all.

∽

I finished with one destroyed and one damaged, which I would sometimes, among the unknowing, elevate to a probable, never more; to do that would be soiling the very thing fought for.

When I returned to domestic life I kept something to myself, a deep attachment—deeper than anything I had known—to all that had happened. I had come very close to achieving the self that is based on the risking of everything, going where others would not go, giving what they would not give. Later I felt I had not done enough, had been too reliant, too unskilled. I had not done what I set out to do and might have done. I felt contempt for myself, not at first but as time passed, and I ceased talking about those days, as if I had never known them. But it had been a great voyage, the voyage, probably, of my life.

I would have given anything, I remember that. The moments of terror—alone, separated from the leader, and seeing, like a knell, drop tanks with their foreign shape and thin, vaporous trails falling silent to both right and left—the sometimes ominous briefings and preparation, the dark early mornings which for me were the worst—none of it mattered. A few years afterwards I won a gunnery championship in North Africa and led an acrobatic team—I had in short, learned equitation. We dropped from the sky into distant countries and once in a while in a locker room or bar I would hear a remark that someone, a name from those days, had been killed in a flying accident, but like Conrad's shipmates on the *Narcissus,* I never saw any of them again.

III.

During the years 1954—1957, Salter was stationed in Europe at Bitburg, an airbase in Germany. They flew from there and also, at times, from fields in France, the Netherlands, Morocco, and Libya. Life was both routine and uneven. This was his last posting as a regular officer.

ভ

In those days there was nothing in the world but us. The rarity was fine. There were other squadrons, of course. Some you knew quite well. Ships from all three squadrons in the group and also from other fields came in past the little shack on wheels by the side of the runway. Many times it is you yourself who are returning, coming back beneath the clouds, seeing the long straight runway, or the hangars alongside it blurring in the rain—an incomparable happiness, the joy of coming home.

ভ

We had pilots named Homer and Ulysses, country boys unfrivolous by nature who took good care of their cars. Farm boys, for some reason, always seemed the truest men. They were even-tempered and unhurried in the way of someone who will watch a man doing something foolish and not make any comment—the joke will come at the end. They became flyers instead of going to the city though of course it was not the same thing, and they saw the world from a distance—the Grand Canal like a gray thread winding among the barely distinguishable piazzas far below, the unmistakable narrowing spire of Paris rising above the haze. Beneath them passed all the miracles of Europe, few of great interest—their wonders were more elemental, in a room, standing naked with a member like a grazing horse's, in front of a full-length mirror with a German whore. Some married waitresses.

You knew them, that is to say their ability and to an extent their character, but much was hidden. After two or three years you knew little more than at the start, but still you were attached to their silence, the honesty of their thoughts. One night one of them, on a motorcycle, sped into the concrete pillar of a bridge and was in the hospital for weeks, legs broken, jaw bound together with silver wire. Nevertheless when I came into the room he managed to smile. He had a willing nature and the name of an ace, strange and abrupt: Uden. Broad and capable hands, fearless eyes, yet somehow it all came to nothing. Face-to-face for the last time at the noisy farewell party, the blue, farm-country eyes suddenly filled with tears. "I know I've disappointed you."

Squadron party in quarters at Bitburg: Salter's wife,
Ann, himself, and Mary Hall Lee whose husband,
M/G Robert Lee, commanded 12th AF

"That's true."

"I just wanted you to know one thing—I won't do it the next time."

That was true also. There was no next time. A year later someone was describing an accident at Myrtle Beach, a night takeoff with full fuel load, 450-gallon drop tanks, the planes wallowing, the overcast seamlessly black. The join-up was in the sky undivided between the darkness of the air and water, a sky without top or bottom; in fact there was no sky, only total blackness in which, banking steeply to try and catch up with the lights of the fleeing leader, the number-three man, low in the roaring nightmare, determined to do well, went into the sea. Uden.

∽

Experience counted, and day-to-day performance. Pilots with few flying hours, in the early years of their career, were the most dangerous. They were young, in the well-being of ignorance, like flies on a sunny table, unaware of the fate of countless others.

∽

With a lanky, indecisive lieutenant named Kelly, I left Bitburg late one day bound for Marseille. Destination weather was forecast to be scattered clouds and eight miles' visibility. I had put him in the lead. It was important to give pilots the chance to make decisions, gain confidence.

Over Marseille at thirty-five thousand feet we had just under eighteen hundred pounds of fuel remaining. The field, Marignane, was not visible. It was hidden by a deck of clouds that had moved in unexpectedly from the sea. In addition, neither Marignane nor Marseille Control would answer our calls.

The sun had already set and the earth was dimming. Kelly signaled for speed brakes and we dove towards a corner of the great lagoon that lay east of the field. We leveled out at three hundred feet. Ahead, like a dark reef, were the clouds. Squeezed as we were into a narrow layer of vanishing light and haze—the bottom of the overcast was perhaps a hundred feet above us—we missed the field. Suddenly the ground began to rise; it disappeared in the clouds just ahead, and we pulled up, breaking out on top at two thousand feet. It had grown darker. I looked at the fuel gauge: a thousand pounds. Kelly seemed hesitant and we were at the threshold of real difficulty.

"I've got it," I said. "Get on my wing." I could hear something he could not, the finality of the silence in which we found ourselves, in which the sole sound was that of the Marignane radio beacon—I rechecked the call letters against my letdown book, FNM.

I turned immediately towards the beacon and examined the letdown diagram. The light was dim. The details were complex—I noted only the heading to the field from the beacon, and the distance and time to fly. At 175 knots this was a minute and twenty-seven seconds.

When things do not go as planned and the fuel gauge is slowly going down, there is a feeling of unreality, of hostile earth and sky. There comes a point when the single fuel needle is all you think about, the focus of all concern. The thought of bailing out of two airplanes over Marseille because we could not find the field in low clouds and darkness was making me even more precise. It was the scenario for many accidents. Did

I have the right frequency and beacon? I checked again. It was right. A moment later, for the first time, the tower came on the air. I suspected they had been waiting for someone to arrive who could speak English. Talking to them, although they were hard to understand, gave me relief: the field was open; there were lights.

We passed over the beacon at two thousand feet, turned to the reciprocal of the field heading and flew for thirty seconds. It seemed minutes. The world was thundering and pouring out. I was determined to do everything exactly, to make a perfect approach. We began a procedure turn—forty-five degrees to the left, hold for one minute, turn back in. The direction-finding needle was rigid. It began to quiver and then swung completely around as we hit the beacon.

We started to descend. The minimum altitude for the field was eight hundred feet, minimum visibility a mile and a half. At five hundred feet we were still in the clouds. Four hundred. Suddenly the ground was just beneath us. The visibility was poor, less than a mile. I glanced at the fuel gauge: six hundred pounds.

A minute had passed. The second hand of the clock was barely moving. A minute and five seconds. A minute ten. Then ahead, like distant stars, faint lines of them, the lights of the field. Speed brakes out, I signaled. Gear and flaps down. We landed smoothly together in the dark.

A taxi drove us into town. We talked about what had happened, what might have. It was not an incident; it was nothing; routine. One flight among innumerable. We could find no place to eat. We slept in a small hotel on a tree-lined street and left early in the morning.

∽

How well one remembers that world, the whiff of jet exhaust, oily and dark, in the morning air as you walk to where the planes are parked out in the mist.

Soon you are up near the sun where the air is burning cold, amid all that is familiar, the scratches on the canopy, the chipped black of the instrument panel, the worn red cloth of the safety streamers stuffed in a pocket down near your shoe. From the tailpipe of the leader's plane comes an occasional dash of smoke, the only sign of motion as it streaks rearwards.

Below, the earth has shed its darkness. There is the silver of countless lakes and streams. The greatest things to be seen, the ancients wrote, are sun, stars, water, and clouds. Here among them, of what is one thinking? I cannot remember but probably of nothing, of flying itself, the imperishability of it, the brilliance. You do not think about the fish in the great, winding river, thin as string, miles below, or the frogs in the glinting ponds, nor they of you; they know little of you, though once, just after takeoff, I saw the shadow of my plane skimming the dry grass like the wings of god and passing over, frozen by the noise, a hare two hundred feet below. That lone hare, I, the morning sun, and all that lay beyond it were for an instant joined, like an eclipse.

One night in early spring there were two of us—I was wingman. No one else was flying at the time. We were landing in formation after an instrument approach. It was very dark, it had been raining, and the leader misread the threshold lights. We crossed the end of the runway high and touched down long. In exact imitation I held the nose high, as he did, to slow down, wheels skipping along the concrete like flat stones on a lake. Halfway down we lowered the noses and started to brake. Incredibly we began to go faster. The runway, invisible and black, was covered with the thinnest sheet of ice. Light rain had frozen sometime after sundown and the tower did not know it. We might, at the last moment, have gone around— put on full power and tried to get off again—but it was too close. We were braking in desperation. I stop-cocked my engine—shut it off to provide greater air resistance—and a moment later he called that he was doing the same. We were standing on the brakes and then releasing, hard on and off. The end of the runway was near. The planes were slithering, skidding sideways. I knew we were going off and that we might collide. I had full right rudder in, trying to stay to the side.

We slid off the end of the runway together and went about two hundred feet on the broken earth before we finally stopped. Just ahead of us was the perimeter road and beyond it, lower, some railroad tracks.

When I climbed out of the cockpit I wasn't shaking. I felt almost elated. It could have been so much worse. The duty officer came driving up. He looked at the massive, dark shapes of the planes, awkwardly placed near each other, the long empty highway behind them, the embankment ahead. "Close one, eh?" he said.

∽

At midday, silvery and slow, the courier floated down the final approach and then skimmed for a long time near the ground getting ready to touch. Nose pointed high, it taxied in. Phipps went to meet it. He stood off to one side and watched it swing around, the grass quivering behind and pebbles shooting off the concrete. When the engines died he walked up and waited for the door to open. There was mail, spare parts, and one passenger, a second lieutenant wearing an overcoat. His baggage was handed down. It turned out he was joining the squadron. "This is the 44th, right?"

"Yeah, this is it. We'll, you're lucky."

"What do you mean?"

"Nothing," Phipps said. "It's just what they told me."

The new man's name was Cassada. He was Phipp's height with hair a little fairer and combed back, Anglo style. Phipps helped him carry his bags while being careful not to be too responsive to questions. Cassada was looking around as they walked. Were these their planes, he wanted to know. Were pilots assigned a plane? Were their names painted on them? Phipps answered yes.

"I'll take you over to meet Captain Isbell," he said.

"Is he the squadron commander?"

"Who, Captain Isbell? No, he's ops."

"Oh," Cassada said.

He was just out of flying school but he'd served as an enlisted man for two years before. He didn't look that old.

∽

It was Friday night, the night for drinking. It would go on for hours. Isbell sat, not really listening, his gaze moving over the crowd, casual but searching, he was not sure for what. True comrades perhaps. Even friends.

Who among them, then, Isbell wondered, someone nearly overlooked, silent and reflective, or another, arguing and intense? Godchaux—he was what it was all about. Grace. The best pilots. Across the room, wedged between men he did not know, was the new one. Fair hair, eyebrows almost joined in the middle. Never trust a man when they come together, they say. As good a rule as any, and the new man, taking it all in, just beginning to select a few idols, Isbell could have picked them out himself, the false glitter.

He emptied his glass and raised a finger for another. It was curious. There were times when he could see them in an entirely different way, for what they were, full of simple courage and youth. Godchaux had a smile that even death would not erase. Dumfries, that idiot, smooth-cheeked and smiling, he had something, too, decent and admirable. There were times when Isbell trusted them all. They were bound together, all of them, he and Dunning too in a great orbit, coming deceptively close to the rest of life and then swinging away. At the extremities were North Africa where they went for gunnery once or twice a year and at the other end the skies of England where great mock battles were sometimes fought. The rest was at home in the Rhineland, rumor, routine, occasional deployments, Munich now and then. They toured the Western world together, stopping at Rome to refuel, Socked in? Divert to Naples—watch the olive trees if you land to the west. Something was usually beginning before the last thing ended. Isbell's true task was biblical. It was the task of Moses—he would take them to within sight of what was promised, but no further. To the friezes of heaven, which nobody knew were there.

༺ঞ༻

"What if both hydraulic systems go out?" Cassada wanted to know.

"That's bad," Grace said.

"Can you move the controls at all?"

Grace shook his head. He had a broad, smooth face and close-cropped hair.

"Not even using the trim?"

"No," Grace said.

Hearts was the game of choice. It showed your true character. Godchaux had the lead, the last trick lay faceup in front of him. Two hearts had fallen in it, the ace and nine. It was Harlan's ace. Ferguson was chanting, "Smoke, smoke."

"Shooting?" Harlan asked.

"Yeah, sure I am," Godchaux said. He tapped his fingers on the back of his cards.

"Well, is there anything else you can do?" Cassada wanted to know. He had confidence in Grace. He was in no position not to have, but still. "Can you do anything?"

"That's what you carry a small screwdriver for," Grace said. "You have one, don't you?"

"No."

"You'd better get one before we go up."

"You mean you can do something in the cockpit?"

"That's right. You unscrew the clock."

"The clock?"

"For a souvenir. Just put it in your pocket and bail out."

∽

To the east it was becoming light, a great, forlorn light that seemed to sweep in from the steppes. The air was still, a sealike calm. He laid his parachute against one of the wheels and began to walk around the airplane, starting at one wing and then following the fuselage to the tail, running a hand over the chilly skin as he went, sometimes patting it like a horse as if to calm it. He was entering the realm of his true authority. He had barely finished the walk-around when the horn sounded. He saw Cassada running out the door, pulling on his gloves as he went, the blare of the horn flooding around him, the crewmen coming after.

Quickly Isbell pulled on his parachute and climbed into the cockpit, fumbling for the safety-belt buckles. The horn kept blowing in panic. The high whine of the engines starting began.

Off on the first scramble, early in the day, no finer time, cold and quiet, the smoke coming straight up from the towns. Munich was blue, deserted. The roads seemed dusted with chalk. The trains were running empty, the streetcars.

At altitude it was silent. The controller directed them north. Serene, pure as angels they flew. At Ingolstadt some clouds began, a thin, floating fence that went up towards

Berlin, gray as a river. Cassada was in position just where he was meant to be, off to the left, looking past Isbell towards the sun and the unknown east. It was there the enemy lay, sometimes inactive, sometimes flying themselves on a parallel course waiting for the slightest violation of the invisible border, or lurking below the contrails, unseen. The controller would call them out but not always, and when the ground was covered by clouds there was always the slight chance of error, a mistake in position or which radar blip was which. The threat of the unexpected was always there. Come and get us, Isbell thought to himself. We're here in the open, alone. Bring us down. Try.

There was nothing, though. No targets, the controller advised. They flew almost to Frankfurt and then turned back. Cassada's plane went from black, to gun color, to silver as he swung from one side to the other in the brilliant light.

They had spoken hardly a word. The earth lay immense and small beneath them, the occasional airfields white as scars. Down across the Rhine. The strings of barges, smaller than stitches. The banks of poplar. Then a city, glistening, struck by the first sun. Stuttgart. The thready streets, the spires, the world laid bare.

∽

I flew south one day, a hundred or two hundred miles into the desert, the earth changing from ruggedness to orange dust.

There was no life, no roads, no trace of anything. Turning, I began to descend in long, uninquisitive arcs until finally, at fifty or a hundred feet, I was heading back north.

At that height one can see only a few miles ahead. Unexpectedly, things began to appear, occasional lonely shepherds, grazing camels, a low, dark group of tents. Suddenly there were animals scattering before me, children throwing themselves to the ground, the momentary glimpse of women who had hurried to tent doors. In twenty minutes I would be on the ground at Wheelus but I would remain aloft much longer in the minds of these unknown people, crossing their world with furious sound and then gone.

～

Isbell walked back to where Cassada was standing. People were still coming out of the club. There was the sound of a woman's heels on the cement. It was too dark to see.

"Who was that, Colonel Neal? He seemed pretty happy," Cassada said.

"Famous figure."

"Why is that?"

"You know how old he is?" Isbell said.

"No."

"Thirty-four."

"Is that all?"

"He was one of the first men in his class to make bird."

They were alone in the darkness, beneath the stars.

"Major Dunning's older than that," Cassada remarked.

"Well, that happens, too. But he's in line for a promotion. His record's good."

"How old are you, Captain?"

"Thirty-one," Isbell said.

Cassada shook his head a little.

"It's a long pull, isn't it?" he said.

"Not for everybody," Isbell replied.

"Colonel Neal."

"He's not the only one."

"You'll get a squadron next."

"I might. I hope so. Not here. I'll be going home too soon. In the States, maybe."

"Well, let me know. I'd like to be in it," Cassada said.

"I'll come looking for you."

The bus came rattling up, headlights quivering before it. It was filled with airmen and NCOs. Isbell stood with Cassada in the back, at the end of a line of lolling heads and the slow reveal of faces as they passed a streetlight. A sergeant was talking. "Lieutenant," he recited, "I loaded them myself, that's what I told him." He had a hard, lined face. Isbell could see him as they went by the hospital.

"You know what he says to me? He says, Bonney, that's good enough for me. That's good enough for me, he says. I tell you, that means something when they talk to you like that."

The others were listening, turned sideways in the seats or leaning from above, holding on with one hand.

"I seen a lot of them," Bonney said, "but I'll tell you one thing, he's the finest."

"No."

"The finest."

"The colonel is."

"Not as a gunner. As an officer, yeah. Not as a gunner."

"Every way."

"No, no. Hell, man, just look at the scores."

"The scores ain't everything."

"Oh, yeah? What else is there?"

"They ain't everything."

They were going down the unlit stretch along the beach. The water was invisible, the color of the night. They rocked along like commuters, the axles squeaking. Cassada's head was bent down as if in thought, but his eyes were open. The light struck his cheekbones. Isbell was remembering, for no reason, the day he had come around the corner of the hangar with the flying suit wet and stuck to him and unwilling to go back and change. How for a moment, before knowing anything, Isbell had thought: this one's different.

"Listen," the sergeant said, "I was in Vegas close to three years. I seen them all."

"Oh, yeah? You remember the one took all the trophies at the meet there a couple of years back? That West Point major?"

"Sure. I know him. He's a real hotshot."

"What's his name again?"

"I know him," the sergeant said. "I seen him shoot."

"You think Lieutenant Piebes could beat him?"

"Hell, yes, he could."

"He ain't that good."

"You want to know what he told me about how he learned shooting?"

"What?"

"I was talking to him the other day and he said, Bonney, I learnt it from flying the tow ship."

"From what?"

"From flying the tow ship, he said."

"Hell, Bonney."

"No, that's right. That's right. It's like a caddie learns how to play golf." He looked around. "How do you think they learn? By watching good golfers, that's how."

He was searching for someone in the dark of the bus, squinting.

"Hey, Lieutenant," he said to Isbell. Then, moving his head a little, "What is it? Captain. I'm sorry. Listen, tell them, isn't that right, that the way to learn is to watch somebody doing it who really knows how."

"That's one way."

"There you are," he cried.

"He didn't say it was the best way."

"You heard the captain. I didn't say nothing about the best way. It don't have to be the best way. The best way is different for everybody, right, Captain?"

Isbell nodded.

Coming to the officers' area, the bus slowed down. When it stopped, Isbell and Cassada jumped off. The door groaned shut and like a battered metal curtain the side of the bus slid past them. They crossed towards their tent. Only the colonel's was noisy. Many people were asleep, ready for departure the next day. Off for Rome or Marseilles, the first leg home.

"What time do you plan to take off?" Cassada asked.

"Let's get going early. Right after breakfast."

"I hate to leave here," Cassada said.

"Maybe you picked up a thing or two."

"Sergeant Bonney. I don't know how much he really knows, but he wasn't that far off."

"It was a good week."

"This was the best thing that's happened to me since I've been in the squadron."

☙

Already lay Valence, half in sunlight, half in shadow, gray against white with touches of gold. They were still climbing, passing twenty-five thousand. Off to the left was an autumn sun in the light of which Cassada's contrail gleamed, a late sun, emptied of heat. Long, clear rays. A sun that infused the canopy like crystal. Isbell could see the minute scratches in the Plexiglas and in the rosy brown of his visor, unexpectedly, a huge eye, the size of a plum, his own. Moist pupil, dark watery iris, lashes. It was staring at something, unwary, intent. At itself.

He looked down towards the earth again and watched the line of the first clouds that, very low, divided Valence in two. Slowly all of it disappeared beneath the nose of the plane. The clouds were a vast glacier extending in all directions as far as he could see. Behind, like a departed shore, the last sight of the earth fell away. Brown hills were vanishing, a thin, polished river. Still in a climb they flew towards Lyons.

The clouds deepened as they went, the tops mounting. At thirty-five thousand Isbell leveled off. The tops were about twenty—it was difficult to say because they weren't solid though they looked it at first. There were large breaks in them. There were shaftways and passages. Milky rays of sunlight shot along them revealing caverns, abysses.

Nearing Lyons the needle of the radio compass began to waver. It fell off halfway, returned, then swung completely around. Isbell watched it, listening to the steady tone of the beacon and thinking not so much of the distance ahead but of how far they had come and how long a way it was back. The cockpit had become white with little stars of frost, as exact as if they had been etched in the glass.

The sun fell lower. It was in the last quarter of its elevation, the light flat. The white of the clouds had faded like an old wall. Everything seemed silent and still as they headed towards Dijon. There was a strange, lost feeling, as though they were in an empty house, in rooms without furniture, looking through windows that had no glass. The world seemed abandoned. The last being had vanished from earth. There were ghostly cities below, desolate highways, meadows bathed in dead light. He had the map unfolded across his lap, looking ahead, listening to nothing. One lone sound reassured him, steady, unending, the sound of the engine, closer to him than breathing, more familiar than his heart.

∽

"You want the latest weather?" There was something more that could not be made out.

"Roger."

"Say again?"

"Roger. The latest weather. The latest weather," Isbell said.

He could hear Cassada transmitting but not clearly. There was a long silence. He began to be uneasy. It was hard to wait. They were traveling seven or eight miles each minute. The sun had sunk lower and a different cast was coming over the sky. In the distance, purples were appearing, the last faint reds. He looked to the east. There, past Italy, were the pillars of night, the deep, welling blues following in the wake of the sun, crossing the invisible Alps, darkening tidelike the clouds of Salzburg, Munich.

"Did you get that?" he heard.

"Negative."

"Did you get the weather, Lead?"

"Negative, negative," Isbell said.

"I can't read you. It's five hundred overcast and two miles . . . ." There was something else, unintelligible.

"What do they have at Chaumont?"

"I can't read you at all. You're very weak and garbled."

Isbell repeated his transmission four or five times. Finally he was understood. He waited. They were past Chaumont by then. The sun was just above the top deck of clouds. The quiet was unnerving. There was an immense, long silence. Time slowed. The minutes grew.

Isbell heard nothing more. His radio was dead, there was not even a side tone. He switched from one channel to another, trying to call or hear anybody. There was nothing. *Five hundred and two,* he was thinking, trying to consider it calmly. The sun was just touching the clouds, tangent to the highest layer, turning it dark as if an act were ending. They had been flying more than an hour. *Five hundred and two.*

He looked out at Cassada and began rocking his wings. He looked at the map. It was more than four hundred miles back to Marseilles. Cassada hadn't moved. Isbell rocked his wings again. Cassada banked gently in towards him. He watched him curve in slowly, the white wake bending, and slide perfectly to Isbell's wingtip.

Isbell passed a hand in front of his face two or three times and touched the side of his helmet. He saw Cassada nod. He tapped his oxygen mask. Another nod. Transmitter and receiver both out. He was still turning things over in his mind. They were only ten or fifteen minutes out. He could feel Cassada waiting, watching, wondering perhaps, though able to talk to the ground. *I'm going to touch down right beside you.* It would be the reverse. Finally Isbell pointed a finger at him, then pointed straight ahead. Cassada's ship moved forward.

Isbell was now flying wing. In the silence he hung there. All that remained in the world was the other airplane. He stared at it. Every detail was terrifically clear. He read the black numbers on the tail. He watched the other plane move, rising slightly, sinking, as if borne by the calmest sea. It seemed incredibly heavy against the sky. He watched Cassada's head move, nod— he was talking to someone—then looked this way and that. What was he saying? What were they telling him? Isbell began switching channels again, fumbling blindly for the set which was behind his left elbow. He called on each frequency, aching to hear something. He saw then that they had started to descend. He glanced at the clouds beneath. They were dark, profound.

They were at twenty thousand, the station still ahead. A thousand years had passed since Marseilles. Isbell glanced quickly at the needle. It was steady. They were close. It was holding dead on as if anchored. When he looked again it had begun to waver, darting from side to side. Speed brakes, he thought, and almost at that moment saw Cassada give the hand signal. In unison they put them out. The noses pitched down. The attitude steepened.

At twelve thousand feet they began the turn to come back inbound. The cloud tops were streaming just beneath them, the threatening gray domes. Cassada's wingtip lights came on. Isbell reached for his own, the panel lights also. Ten thousand feet. In a bank. The clouds were skimming below. In a silence that existed for Isbell alone they went down together towards the hidden earth.

∽

Get us on, Isbell was thinking, get us on. They were trying the third time but everything was running the wrong way, he could feel it, a tide in the dark pulling at his legs. Get us on. He was either saying or thinking it when suddenly they came skimming out of the clouds in the moment of revelation, his heart rising up into his throat.

This time he saw it all. They had come down even lower, a hundred feet off the ground, bursting in and out of the ragged scud. Instants of vision, then into it again. The runway, the yellow mobile, everything passing by on the left as he saw it was like the others, no good. There welled up in him without thinking, oh, God, and looking down for a second too long he was late as Cassada turned. He turned hard himself, following, watching the ship ahead, the ground, clouds, the control tower almost straight on. Then Cassada was gone into a cloud lower than the rest. Isbell was in trail. He would see Cassada on the other side in a moment. Two moments. Longer. The cloud did not end. They never emerged. Isbell was on his own instruments, climbing. The tops were far above. The bases were frightening. He was climbing alone.

He was unable to think. He didn't know what heading he was on. It meant nothing just then. He was watching the fuel gauge. They were sometimes off by a couple hundred pounds. On top, he was thinking, on top. He could not concentrate on anything but that. The brightness above. To circle for a moment there within sight of the sky. He did not know whether there was something else he might be doing or not. He had to climb.

It became a little easier the higher he went. The airplane was flying as if it could go on forever. It was powerful, light. He didn't wonder about Cassada, where he had gone. There was nothing left but a silent, darkening world, rock-hard, waiting for him to fall. He looked again at the fuel gauge. He was unable to keep his eyes from it, no matter how hard he tried.

∽

In his mind Isbell prepares it. The details merge, become entangled. He forces his way through them, striving to make them distinct. He watches the instruments as he climbs, it seems to take a minute to read each one. A hundred and fifty pounds. He has made the decision but cannot move. He sits frozen, trying to believe.

Twenty-five hundred feet. He is delaying but can't think why. At any moment there'll be a surge, the gauges dying then coming back. The expectation makes him hollow. His hand won't move. He looks down at the red handle that blows the canopy. He can't touch it. The first, warning lurch will make him jump like a cat but he does nothing. The engine is steady, the plane intact.

One hundred pounds. The agony of the end. With an abrupt movement he levels the wings. He was rolling into a bank unaware. Pull it now, he thinks. Then sit erect. Squeeze the forked handles. He knows it from a thousand recitations. Pull. He can't.

The safety pin. Suddenly he thinks of that and looks down. It's out. Three thousand feet. Should he begin slowing? The clouds are a death shroud. He is climbing for the last time, sick, clinging to a dream that is over. The cockpit lights gleam in the glass above his head. Fifty pounds. He levels off and reduces power. He feels nothing. He is a ghost who is flying. Then in an instant that passes. He thinks: I have to do it now. I have to move my hands.

He tries. They glide across his lap, independent, light. The left takes the stick. The right drops down and takes hold of the handle, round in his palm. He tightens his fingers and gathers himself. Ready. Pull!

Nothing happens. His hand will not do it. It's like trying to pull out a tooth. Mechanically, like a child, he starts counting. One . . . two . . . The next word jams. He begins again, resolute. One . . . Two . . . A pause. Three! He yanks up. The air explodes, icy, vast. The canopy is gone. A roaring surrounds him. He almost feels regret. Scraps of paper flash by. The maps inflate, rise past him and are torn away. The wind is tearing at his clothes. I've done it, he thinks! The relief is so great he could laugh.

Suddenly he feels a heave. The ship hesitates for a moment and goes forward again. He can't make out the instruments. It doesn't matter. He could smash them with a hammer, break everything. All is profaned, all is going and at any moment, a terminal sounding, fierce and ultimate. The death dive. Get out, he thinks. He realizes he can't tell what attitude it's taking. He might be rolling over, blind, out of control. Get out!

He sits there trying to think. He has hold of the forked ejection grip and is beginning to squeeze when there's another hesitation, mortal, abrupt. A surge as the engine catches again. The last of the fuel. He forces his head back against the heavy plate, tenses his legs bringing them close, and before he knows what has happened, with a shock, a hunching jolt, his fist holding the two leaves tight together, he is gone, through the darkness, into the black air.

∽

There are wandering lights and soon the first pieces on the ground.

"Here's something," Godchaux calls.

He picks it up. Cadin's flashlight plays on it. Impossible to say what it is. A metal shard. Perhaps part of a hydraulic cylinder—it has a sticky sheen.

A trail of debris begins. There is ammunition scattered on the ground, some of it linked together, the rest strewn like teeth. Then a large piece, one of the gun-bay panels. The drop tanks. Cadin stands, moving the beam back and forth over a large section of wing. Harlan kicks at something, stoops and picks it up gingerly.

"Shine it this way, Colonel."

The first ominous chord. It's a shoe. Harlan holds it slightly away from himself and turns it so he can see inside.

"It's empty."

He places it alongside his own foot. It's smaller.

Twenty feet farther on there is something pale floating in a small puddle. Godchaux reaches down. The water is deeper than it looks. He pulls up a map, soggy and dripping, a course drawn on it in grease pencil. There are other scraps of paper around, pages from the maintenance forms. At the edge of some woods they come to the end of it. The emblem of disaster, the engine, huge, with dirt packed into it, is at the base of a tree, the trunk marked with a great, white gouge.

They stand, looking over the scene.

"I don't see the seat anywhere," Dunning says.

"No."

It may be elsewhere, part of an ejection.

"We ought to work back."

"Yes," the colonel agrees. "Spread out more."

Feet soaked, they walk through the rain, moving slowly. Ahead are two or three lights jerking from spot to spot on the ground. The sky is invisible, absolutely black. It's like being in a mine or a deep, underground cave. They stumble over rocks. Then Harlan calls,

"Over here!"

The flashlight glides to something, hard to make out.

"Here's the cockpit," Harlan says.

The flashlight stays on it, then other lights as searches converge. The seat is lying on its side, ripped free. It's empty. Cadin's light moves to a section of the instrument panel and picks out the black gauges. Harlan is bending over something a few feet away.

"What is it?"

"Canopy frame," he says.

They look at the seat again. The safety belt is unbuckled. Dunning tries to calculate what that might mean. The ejection handle hasn't been raised. The seat wasn't fired.

"That's where we found him," somebody says.

Cadin's light comes up and holds there. It's a corpsman, white uniform visible beneath a raincoat. He wears a pair of rubber boots.

"Dead?" Cadin says.

The corpsman nods. "Yes, sir."

The cold is making them shiver. Rain runs down their faces. Dunning has borrowed a flashlight and goes off by himself, poking his way from piece to piece, making small, slow circles at his feet with the light. He stops and then goes on, aimlessly it seems. He is gathering the catastrophe, wandering in it like a sleepwalker. The wreckage is total. Nothing can recombine it.

∞

In formation with Minish one day, coming back from a mission, I on his wing—without a word he pulled up and did an Immelmann, I as close as you can get, then another and another, then some loops and rolls, two or three away from me, all in hot silence, I had not budged a foot, the two of us together, not a word exchanged, like secret lovers in some apartment on a burning afternoon.

❧

Munich for the last time, glittering in the darkness, immense—
the shops, the avenues, the fine cars. The wingman's ship is out
to one side near a crescent moon. The Arend-Roland comet is
visible, its milky tail flying southwards for thousands of miles,
an inch in the sky. I lean back and gaze at it, my helmet against
the padding. I will never see it again or, just this way, all that is
below. Some joys exist in retrospect but not this, the serenity,
the cities shining in detailed splendor. From the deeps of the
sky we look down as if upon our flocks.

❧

The Air Force—I ate and drank it, went in whatever weather
on whatever day, talked its endless talk, climbed onto the wing
to fuel the ship myself, fell into the wet sand of its beaches
with sweaty others and was bitten by its flies, ignored wavering
instruments, slept in dreary places, rendered it my heart.

❧

I sat at a desk in Separations and typed out my letter; then,
like the survivor of some wreck, I roamed, carrying it, through
the corridors for more than an hour. Finally I saw a colonel I
knew, Berg, coming out of the doorway. He worked in Person-
nel, in charge of promotion boards. Needing the confidence of
someone, I told him what I was about to do. He mentioned

[James Salter]

several other officers who had recently resigned. I found it of little comfort. Late in the afternoon, feeling almost ill, I handed in the letter. It was the most difficult act of my life.

∽

Never another city, over it for the first time, in the lead, the field that you have never landed on far below, dropping down towards it, banking steeply one way, then the other, calling the tower, telling them who you are. Never another sunburned face in Tripoli looking up at you as you taxi to a stop, the expression asking, ship OK? A thumb raised, OK. And the dying whine, like a great sigh, of the engine shutting down, the needles on the gauges collapsing. It is over.

IV.

Years when I crossed the country alone, like some replica Philip Nolan, in thousand-mile legs. Taking off from Wright-Patterson in a tremendous rainstorm, unable to even see the end of the runway or the trees. Taking off at March and Forbes. Taking off at Tyndall, the earth like dust on a mirror, a long, unmoving line of smoke—from the paper mill, was it?—running south as far as the eye could see. Going out early in the morning, hands still numb, the magical silence of the runways, the whole pale scene. Heading for the Gulf under its blue haze, counties and parishes intent and unaware though I know their lives in vast detail, Brookley shining like a coin in the light off Moblie Bay.

Sometimes, because of the light, in the visor there is the

moist dark of one's own eye, bigger than a movie poster. Sometimes there is the sun directly ahead making it impossible to read the instruments. The earth below is shadowed. There are mythic serpents of water, lakes, rivers smooth as marble. Empty sky, the rumbling aircraft, the radio overflowing with voices and sounds. Above the yellow horizon, near the vanishing sun, suddenly, a dot. Behind it a faint line, a contrail. By some forgotten reflex I am stunned awake, as in days past when we watched intently, when the body filled with excitement to see it: the enemy!

∾

One night as I was calling for a letdown near St. Louis, the city jewel-like and clear, a voice in the darkness asked, "Flatfoot Red, is that you?" Flatfoot, our call sign from Bitburg, and Red, the color of the lead flight.

"Yes," I said. "Who's that?"

En route you seldom saw other fighters and almost never recognized a voice.

"Ed White."

The pleasure, the thrill, in fact, the sort that comes from a lingering glance across a room, a knowing nod, or a pair of fingers touched briefly to the brow. We were able to exchange only a few words—How are you? Where are you headed? I looked for him in the blackness, the moving star that would be his plane, but the heavens were littered with stars, the earth strewn with lights. He was on his way to somewhere, the heights, I was sure. I was going in to land.

"See you," he said.

Who could know it would be otherwise and he was the one whom I would never see again? We had flown on the acrobatic team together, he on the right wing, Whitlow the left, Tracy in the slot.

After his death his widow remarried. Not many years later, she herself died, apparently a suicide. The waters had closed over them both.

ᖆ

The then and now are intertwined, the dimming past and the present. Like an enduring disease there are the dreams. I am flying with someone, wide open, on the deck. The sky is cloudy, the flak terrifying. We are going at top speed, flashing past storage tanks, along a river on the way to the target. Suddenly ahead in the mist, steel bridges! Too late to pull up! We hit them! A great wave of heat sweeps over me. I have crossed—it is completely real—over into death.

I wake in the darkness and lie there. The aftertaste is not bitter. I know, just as in dreams, I will die, like every living thing, many of them more noble and important, trees, lakes, great fish that have lived for a hundred years. We live in the consciousness of a single self, but in nature there seems to be something else, the consciousness of many, of all, the herds and schools, the colonies and hives with myriads lacking in what we call ego but otherwise perfect, responsive only to instinct. Our own lives lack this harmony. We are each of us an eventual tragedy. Perhaps it is only that winter is coming on.